That which was from the beginning,
which we have heard,
which we have seen with our eyes,
which we have looked at
and our hands have touched
— this we proclaim
concerning the Word of life.

1 JOHN 1:1, NIV

EMBODIED FAITH

Reflections on a Materialist Spirituality

Ola Tjørhom

William B. Eerdmans Publishing Company
Grand Rapids, Michigan / Cambridge, U.K.

Published 2009 by
Wm. B. Eerdmans Publishing Co.
2140 Oak Industrial Drive N.E., Grand Rapids, Michigan 49505 /
P.O. Box 163, Cambridge CB3 9PU U.K.

Printed in the United States of America

15 14 13 12 11 10 09   7 6 5 4 3 2 1

Library of Congress Cataloging-in-Publication Data

Tjørhom, Ola.
  Embodied faith: reflections on a materialist spirituality / Ola Tjørhom.
      p.   cm.
  Includes bibliographical references.
  ISBN 978-0-8028-6274-7 (pbk.: alk. paper)
  1. Christian life — Catholic authors. 2. Materialism —
  Religious aspects — Catholic Church.   I. Title.

  BX2350.3.T56   2009
  248.4 — dc22

                        2008051814

www.eerdmans.com

Contents

Contents

Preface

Christian faith should not be confused with subscribing to a fixed set of opinions or religious tenets. Faith is first and foremost life. Or more precisely: It leads us into a full and true life, the life that God originally meant for his creation.

This life is not based on lofty ideas and abstract theories. It is grounded in a concrete space, namely the church. Here it is attached to things we hear and see, smell and taste, as well as to simple acts. It is further lived out in and for God's world, through virtues like charity, solidarity — and plain decency.

By this we have singled out the two central arenas of our faith life, the church and the world. These two spheres are not identical. But they are clearly connected, also in the sense that they presuppose each other mutually. Church and world must thus be seen as interrelated entities. Here the challenge is to keep together what belongs together in God's plan of salvation.

This small book aims at contributing to a picture of how a Christian life can be lived. In my proposal for a viable piety, the concept "materialist spirituality" is at the core. To some this concept may sound paradoxical bordering on senselessness. I shall try to give an explanation of its meaning and implications throughout the succeeding chapters. Here I settle with a brief listing of its main features: Materialist spirituality is sacramentally founded; it is anchored in empirical perception; and it is lived out in our daily lives and the world.

It is important for me to stress that the emphasis on empirical sensation in my outlining of a materialist spirituality does not exclude those who have lost one or more of their senses. Since they in most cases employ remaining senses more strongly, this sort of piety will be accessible to all. Actually, materialist spirituality can be seen as a "democratic" spirituality since it does not require a special religious "antenna system" or a predefined set of "feelings."

The volume's table of contents suggests that a huge number of complex theological issues are touched here. None of these issues will be discussed at full length. They are only considered as building-blocks of a materialist spirituality. Due to the interconnectedness of the central topics of several of the chapters, some repetition has been unavoidable. Generally, the following is not meant as an advanced theological treatise, hence the lack of footnotes. I have settled with listing relevant literature at the end of each chapter. My central aim has been to contribute in establishing a bridge between ecclesiological reflection — which has been at the core of my scholarly work — and our life in Christ as a whole.

I have taught Christian dogmatics for almost three decades. Over the years, the knowledge of the elementary basics of faith among students — and elsewhere — has been steadily declining. This contribution may perhaps also have a certain relevance in this connection. At any rate, there is a clear need of simple and straightforward introductions to the central aspects of Christianity.

Throughout the book, I have included references to contemporary developments in church life, politics, and culture. Such references largely depend on the eyes that see. Further, in a rapidly changing and fluctuating world, there is always a danger that the chosen illustrations will come across as annoyingly outdated. Yet, it belongs to the nature of a materialist spirituality that it is grounded in and related to specific contexts. Anyway, the examples I offer seemed to be clearly relevant to me when I wrote this presentation.

Today we are almost drowning in highly diverse literature on spirituality. Such literature is often preoccupied with exotic and even bizarre factors, turning us into tourists in our approach to religion. This marks some Christian and theological contributions to the genre, too. I have chosen the opposite path. My aim is to outline a far less spectacular, but

— hopefully — more sustainable piety; a piety where we refrain from offering people stones instead of bread. Seen in this perspective, "materialist spirituality" is intended as an alternative to the "spirituality wave." It is also construed as a critical spirituality.

The vast richness of the church's faith deposit across time and space and its "Great Tradition" are a steady and abundant source of spiritual renewal. Here there is no reason to venture into the tedious attempts at reinventing the wheel that mark much contemporary spirituality. There is, however, a clear need to integrate these impulses in our factual existence and current realities. This cannot be achieved through abstruse religious tourism or retrospective nostalgia.

Spirituality concerns our life in the Holy Spirit. It can, thus, to some extent be perceived as "ecclesiology in practice" or "realized ecclesiology." Yet, this requires that the fundamental importance of God's creation is kept in mind and that all forms of narrow and sterile ecclesiocentrism are avoided.

It is now approximately five years since I was received into the full fellowship of the Roman Catholic Church. Even if I write this as a Catholic, I am still fairly new to the craftsmanship of Catholic theology. And I have no illusions of being capable of presenting an even remotely complete or representative introduction to Catholic spiritual life. The subsequent account is personal, but — hopefully — not in any sense private. I simply want to share things that have worked reasonably well for me, wishing that they may be useful for others too.

Developments on the Norwegian church scene and within the Lutheran family at large during the last decades form a central, if more implicit context of my deliberations. Some of these developments contributed to my decision to convert. It should be emphasized, though, that the following is not conceived as a slightly camouflaged conversion narrative. My process here was far too unexciting to merit a book. The succeeding chapters should rather be read as signs of the joy of having full access to the treasures of Catholic spirituality. Simultaneously, all this is written in deep gratitude for what I have learned from different types of Lutheran piety and through ecumenical participation.

In the wake of this, I would like to underscore that I hope materialist spirituality will come across as an ecumenically valid form of piety and, accordingly, as relevant in regard to the exchange on "spiritual ecumenism." My point of departure is the sacramental approach to Christian life that marks various forms of Catholicity, with a particular focus on the concreteness and down-to-earth character of sacramentality. But the Lutheran vocation ethics — partly including its Pietistic and Protestant adaptations — has played a crucial role, too. This is also the case with vital inputs from the Anglican tradition. In my view, these approaches are fully capable of enriching each other mutually. The ecumenical dimension is a key concern in the present volume.

The original version of this account was published in Norway (by Verbum) in 2005. A Swedish translation (by Artos) came the same year. This is an adjusted, expanded and largely new-written edition of the book, also based on constructive responses from readers. The translation is by the author, who does not have English as his mother tongue. I still hope that I have been able to express my concerns in a reasonably transparent way. Let me add that I have used an older edition of the Bible — namely the Revised Standard Version of 1971 — for the simple reason that this edition is most familiar to me.

In preparing the original manuscript, I had the great fortune of receiving advice and encouragement from the Dominican sisters Mildri Hoch-Nielsen, Else-Britt Nilsen, and Anne Bente Hadland of St. Catherine's Convent in Oslo. They did their utmost to keep a still fresh and possibly a bit wavering Catholic faithfully on track. Whenever the sisters have succeeded here, they should have the credit. If their efforts occasionally have failed, I am the only one to blame. I would also like to thank former colleagues at the School of Mission and Theology in Stavanger for valuable help, especially in regard to library services. Thanks also to Kjell Pahr-Iversen — a Norwegian artist of international standing — for permission to use his powerful canvas "Icon" at the front cover of the book, and to Inge Bruland for photographing the image. And I am, of course, ever so grateful to Eerdmans for publishing my deliberations. Without the steadfast support of Managing Editor Linda Bieze there might not have been a book at all.

Most of all I would like to express my deep gratitude to those who — throughout the years and in varying ways — have taught me how our life in Christ can be lived. Such learning is at the core of all ecumenical ventures. Let me, therefore, underline that I welcome contributions that aim at developing the concept of "materialist spirituality" further in a fruitful way.

Ola Tjørhom
Stavanger, Norway
Advent 2008

BACKGROUND AND DEFINITION

1 The Horizon

*Neo-Liberalism, Privatization, and a Blooming
Religious Market Under the Auspices of
"Postmodernity"*

No bid for a viable spirituality is presented in a vacuum. Various factors
and phenomena — not least of a broad cultural and sub-theological nature — exercise a strong influence in this field. Here I shall restrict myself to discussing five such factors: The proclivity towards "market fundamentalism" in contemporary Western or Northern societies — often
being endorsed under the devious label of globalization; an escalating
populism that is fueled largely by market forces; today's deceptively
blooming and kitschy religious market; the massive increase of internalization and privatization within the sphere of religion; and the conspicuous cultural impact of "postmodernism."

I am a theologian — and neither an accomplished politician nor a
prophet. The following is, therefore, not intended as an objective or fully
balanced presentation of the developments of our societies and culture.
The Western European context is the main background of my account.
Parts of it are deliberately provocative. Moreover, political and cultural
realities keep changing so rapidly that few individuals have sufficient insight to pass definite judgments here. Yet, the following reflections are vital in appreciating the wider, more negative horizon of a "materialist spirituality." And they affirm that such piety must include a *critical* approach.

The basic idea of religion — and especially of the Christian faith
— is not that we shall flee from reality, but rather that we shall be enabled to cope with it in a sensible and responsible manner. Furthermore: Without a proper relationship to the world, there is no true spirituality. At this point, the fluffy neo-religiosity of the market has little to

3

offer. Something far more solid is required. One would hope that people still will consider authentic Christianity and the "Great Tradition" of the church as vigorous and clearly relevant options here.

Before I consider the wider framework of a materialist spirituality in more detail, I need to underline that these deliberations were written *before* the international financial crisis that emerged during the fall of 2008. Obviously, many things look different when seen in the light of this crisis. And as always, the poor and deprived are hit hardest. At the same time, these events reflect and affirm the enormous vulnerability of pure market ideologies. I have thus chosen to keep the following account unchanged. It may even contribute to an explanation of recent developments in our society.

During the last decades, the market with its anything-but-free forces has been accepted as the key ruling mechanism in almost all sectors of the Northern or Western hemisphere and its satellite states — hence the expression "market fundamentalism." Today similar attitudes are growing within the expanding economies of Russia, China, and India. This creates vast space for a wildly liberalistic ideology that denounces all efforts to control the market as deadly sins. Many of our political leaders seem to adhere to the illusion that excessive buying or spending is a feasible way towards a sustainable society; through the so-called media-revolution we are "amusing ourselves to death" (Neil Postman); our cultural life is dominated by quantitative perspectives and the inevitable desire for fast money; and even our academic institutions are yielding to a market ideology. Also in Christian circles, neo-conservative liberalist sentiments are being embraced in a strikingly uncritical way. The only lingering counterforce appears to be a steadily decreasing and marginalized group of free souls, while the rest of us are busy nourishing our "practical materialism."

A fateful result of the dominance of the market is that a slightly growing number of prosperous people are becoming wealthier — a select few command fortunes of an incredible size, while the vast majority is getting increasingly deprived. The gap between rich and poor has never been larger than today. This is certainly the case in view of the relationship between affluent and struggling nations. However, a similar trend has spread within our societies — including the so-called welfare states. Massive unemployment in Germany, recent miseries among U.S. homeowners, and the culture of greed and voracity that is exposed among top-ranking business executives are examples of this gloomy development.

In addition to this, the economy — the driving force of the market — has undergone significant changes. Previously, it had a largely instrumental function, underpinning and serving the production of goods. Today, the financial sector has assumed an independent and secluded role — ceaselessly catering to its own purposes and expediting its rapid and uncontrolled growth. Here the selling or a ruthless moving around of capital often generates far more profit than dealing in goods. This has led to a "bubble economy" where company values can surge dramatically or drop disastrously overnight. Only those who are callous enough to shift their priorities at exactly the right moment will benefit from these mechanisms, while the vast majority in the long run is doomed to lose — some to the point of bankruptcy. The money industry has thus become an arena for "easy earnings" — hardly paying any attention to values that are beneficial to society at large. This shift has also had a huge impact on corporate culture. To many the crucial thing is to create a more or less sustainable impression of "value potential" and not to deliver in a concrete sense. In my opinion, these developments represent a bigger threat than the yuppie economy of the 1980s. At any rate, the claim that the financial market in its present shape should be granted absolute "freedom" is simply absurd. And it would be disastrous if this economy invaded the public sector, too.

To the extent that minor signs of change have emerged lately, the chief reason is that God's creation is crying out loudly that market fundamentalism — in its more traditional forms as well as its "bubble economy" version — simply cannot be continued. Global warming, frequent natural disasters, and life-threatening pollution are all more or less direct results of an unrestricted market ideology. A constantly high demand on energy as well as a wide selection of consumer goods makes it complicated to organize our economies in a more sensible manner. Our response to these essential challenges is still far too vague and evasive. At present, the illusion of a "free" market is being exported fervently beyond the borders of the Western hemisphere — through blunt financial, political, or military coercion and cynical advertising. For the market can never be satisfied by limited rule; it consistently goes for world dominion.

This indicates that we have made the market forces omnipotent. However, in light of the fundamental conviction that "the customer is always right," the market is more than willing to share its omnipotence with those who possess and cultivate a relentless consumer capacity. And for the first time in history, the really big spender is the people at large — eagerly trying to accommodate to the slogan "Shop till you drop." This has led to a "democratization" of luxury shopping that entices us to spend small fortunes on, say, handbags or ridiculous electronic gadgets. At the same time, we are caught up in a low-price hype in regard to the things we need most — namely food. If we show the least signal of approaching the limits of our ability to consume, banks and other financial establishments have been lining up — at least until now — in order to provide us with credit cards or loans that enable us to continue spending.

The borrowed supremacy of the people has created space for massive populist currents with totalitarian features. Lying on our couches watching TV and eating junk food, we exercise our power by aggressively pestering anyone who tries to contribute to functioning leadership. The people have become their own Big Brother, both in the Orwellian and in the modern media meaning of the term. We live in a time that exposes a desperate need of effective political leadership — in our attempts to regain a healthy environment as well as our endeavors to combat poverty. However, people refuse to accept heteronymous or external direction; they claim all leading positions for themselves. And this is often done on the basis of shortsighted, immature, and purely selfish motives. It is now approximately forty-five years since Pope John XXIII, in his Encyclical *Pacem in Terris*, observed that people are inclined to demand their own rights while forgetting their duties over against their neighbors and society at large. Never has this prophetic observation been more appropriate than today.

Culture is particularly exposed to popular currents. The cultural preferences of the people are marked by an intense urge for phenomena that deliver static confirmation — suggesting that plain recognition has been elevated to the status of revelation. Art that challenges and offers critical perspectives, however, is often met by hysterical reactions bordering on hatred. In this way, we cut ourselves off from critical impulses that have the capacity to promote growth. This also explains the stagnant nature of the popular culture industry.

Increasing uniformity is a key feature of the reigning popular culture. Despite the customary praise of diversity, we invariably — and ironically — seem to end up with just more of the same. Moreover, today's populism is bent on a culture of adolescence. This largely depends on the vast expansion of the youth segment that has occurred during the last few decades; presently we become "babes" and "kids" when we are five or six years old and stay like this until we reach fifty. A third feature of contemporary popular culture is its strong proclivity towards privatization. Here private arenas are divulged to the broad public — some people can hardly wait to open their bedroom doors to just about anyone, while the proper public sphere is being privatized.

Given the dominant position of market fundamentalism, there is no reason to be overly surprised that religion and faith too have become commodities or articles of trade. In past times, spirituality was a concern for the select few. During the last decades, however, it has been popping up in a number of likely and less likely contexts. On the one hand, this implies a positive opportunity for the church. On the other hand, the substance and content of the notion in question have been changed radically in this process — hence, the expression "neo-religiosity." As a consequence of this, the concept of spirituality is now marked by ambiguity and obscurity.

This is clearly affirmed by a glance at our increasingly flourishing and colorful, or kitschy, religious market. In recent years, the selling of spirituality has developed into a huge industry. Seen against this background, one might suggest that God — by many considered to be dead — has risen in the shape of capital. Lately, even a prominent member of the Norwegian royal family has established an enterprise that offers advice and training on how we can get in touch with angels and similar, typically neo-religious hokum. In the marketplace of religion, we encounter a striking and even bizarre mixture of Eastern religiosity and Western popular psychology, fashionable feel-good stuff and rudiments of Christian mysticism. Occasionally, the resulting blend has an almost alchemistic character. But the hazier and stranger it gets, the better it seems to sell. In this connection, I recall a cartoon I once saw that maintained we are called to be "spiritual fruits" and not "religious nuts." And I cannot help having a sad feeling that religious shoppers are being offered stones instead of bread.

Still, people construct their own, highly private beliefs on the basis of their religious shopping — applying ingredients that seen from a logical and historical viewpoint are clearly divergent or even contradictory. In some cases, they behave like more or less infallible theologians — be-

7

ing reluctant to accept any critical reactions or corrective inputs. The central criterion of the selection process is personal well-being, largely disregarding the needs of our neighbors and the world. Here the distinction between faith and cosmetics, spirituality and plastic surgery is obscured. Religion is thus turned into shallow therapy, while healers exercise priestly functions. This suggests that religious consumerism can be just as inconsiderate and self-centered as other types of consumerism.

The current religious sale-winners expose many common characteristics. One such feature is that modern religion often comes across as widely "anthropologized" — meaning that it focuses chiefly on immediate and somewhat trivial human demands. At the same time, God is in danger of being reduced to the level of pure instrumentality or even total oblivion. Formerly people might have considered religious faith as a way of "finding oneself." Today we are more concerned with "constructing" our identity and personality. Through the readily available assistance of myriads of personal coaches, trend experts, and feature journalists, this process is inclined to take us way beyond any conceivable reality. For many, anthropologized religion is conceived mainly as an important building-block in the ongoing construction of their selves, while the essential vertical anchoring of faith is tuned down or even ignored.

Additionally, market spiritualities can be banal in the sense that they disregard or even bluntly deny our capacity for rational reflection. Their inclination towards trivialities is often coupled with a striking pomposity and pretentiousness, unashamedly addressing the big questions of life through tiny and cramped answers. In emphasizing hyper-exotic elements, neo-religious spirituality corresponds to our boundless appetite for entertainment and strong, but unreal experiences or sensations. Moreover, such spirituality is located within a foggy fantasy-landscape where reality and our daily lives are seen as unsolicited digressions. And since the spirituality of the market is directed towards smooth mass consumption, it is totally void of critical perspectives. Right now, hardly anything is more difficult to sell than convictions that incorporate concrete claims in regard to our way of living. This is probably the main reason why the market tends to strip religion of its essential ethical components. In its ardent pursuit of personal well-being and feel-good sentiments, neo-religiosity frequently comes across as morally blind and deaf.

The religious market has also caught up with several Christian groups and churches. At this point, the neo-charismatic movement and the so-called independent "megachurches" have played a leading role. Within these groups, a passionate pursuit of powerful and evocative emotions is at the core. The goal seems to be to provide people — accustomed to a daily diet of beastly murders and sexual offenses on a myriad of TV channels — with even stronger sensations. This leads to a noisy overemphasis on the extraordinary, where outward effects are considered far more important than spiritual contents. Worship is in danger of degenerating into a performance or a show, while the experience spiral is turned higher and higher.

Today, there are signs of a shift of emphasis within the faith movement. An example of this can be found in Rev. Joel Osteen and his Lakewood Church, which worships in Houston's former basketball arena. Here the loud and raucous style of the previous representives of this current has been replaced by polished exteriors and posh Armani suits. Osteen's message — or market strategy — is directed towards the more prosperous middle-class segments. In his poignant sermons he tells us that God wants everyone to be affluent and successful. This is accompanied by hefty tunes from the late Freddy Mercury, "We Are the Champions," which serves as the favorite inspirational anthem at Lakewood. In my opinion, Osteen and his ilk can be seen as a Christian adaptation of the "bubble economy." And while such versions of Christianity sell in buckets, the established churches struggle with stagnation and serious setbacks.

Trying to recover their position, the mainline churches are also exposed to the temptations of the religious market. In Scandinavia there is a tendency to confuse the folk-church concept with the peculiar idea that people "own" the church. Among some it has become fashionable to talk condescendingly about so-called "political correctness." Seen in light of present political realities, I strongly object to this view. Yet, one has to admit that there are cases where such correctness has contributed to what may be characterized as ecclesiological populism — not least in the field of Christian ethics. On the Roman Catholic side, we find a proclivity to succumb to people's urge for religious nostalgia.

Some interpret our booming spirituality market as a sign of religious renaissance. Basically, one might argue that religion has experienced a sort of comeback lately. Still, there is an obvious need to investigate the nature and implications of this return. What comes back is a radically changed religiosity in which populism, a pick-and-choose mentality, and an aesthetic approach provide the framework. A vaguely pictured "beauty" of faith seems to be far more appealing today than its truth contents, let alone its ethical implications. Subsequent to this, the demand for theology and authentic tradition vanishes rapidly. Surely, theology without spirituality is a distressing venture. This is affirmed by the exigent observation of Franz Cardinal König: *Molto teologia, poco Dio* — much theology, but little God. But there are cases where spirituality without theology can be just as bad — or even worse. Generally, the religious market possesses an immense transformative capacity. At this point, the attitude of the churches has frequently been far too naïve.

The success of several types of market spirituality depends heavily on their correspondence and conformity with the religious privatization that has taken place in Western societies over the years — inside as well as outside the church. The U.S. proxy of this largely European feature seems to be religious individualization with roots in puritanism. In spite of continual secularization, people still seem to believe. But they believe in their own manner — and often they believe in the most peculiar things. Quite a few of us are shopping around at the religious market, picking up whatever may have instant appeal. On that basis we construct our own private faith, without being bothered by public religion or inherited creedal systems. What is seen as personal authenticity is considered far more important in this connection than the potential of religion to promote communality and to strengthen bonds of unity within an increasingly divided society. Even the rituals or rites of the church are being tailored in accordance with personal demands these days. This implies that their unifying function is put at jeopardy.

One might think that the ongoing privatization has granted religion a more central role in people's lives. In my view, this is hardly the case. For as already indicated, the spirituality that sells often comes across as strange, bordering on the hyper-exotic. The result of this is that we behave like tourists in our approach to religion. We bustle around, "inspired" by phenomena that have no chance at all of being properly integrated in our lives or in the realities of the world we live in. This probably corresponds with our desire for a religion that does not get too close and bothersome, that can be kept at a convenient distance, that will not interfere too much in our existence. Accordingly, private religion often becomes distant religion.

Especially within pietistic and Protestant traditions, it was claimed that "collective religiosity" is less demanding — and thus less valuable — than personal or heart-based practices. Now, however, this appears to be turned upside down. While privatization and internalization allow us to choose the most convenient type of religion, publicly exercised faith — not least within churches with a strong ecclesiological identity — is experienced as more "costly" or "severe." This is probably a key reason why many today prefer personalized beliefs at the expense of public religion. On a similar note, outward religiosity was in low esteem among Pietists. At present, external manifestations of faith often come across as threatening to the point of being banned. The preeminent example here is the stern reaction against the *hijab* of many Muslim women. However, British Airways also denied a female flight attendant the right to wear a cross while on duty. Developments like these can be interpreted in different ways. But they seem to reflect a growing skepticism over against public and visible faith, particularly in cases where the people concerned are serious about their religion.

Lately, there has been an immense surge in militant fundamentalism — emerging as a horrifyingly visible form of religion. This is not solely a Muslim phenomenon; it clearly occurs among Christians, too — mainly within neo-charismatic and neo-conservative circles. In practice, these hostile currents presuppose and feed on each other mutually. Now, this is not the place for a detailed discussion of fundamentalist attitudes. One thing must be mentioned, though: If I had to choose between fundamentalism and privatized religiosity, I would of course have gone for the latter. Luckily, however, there is a preferable third option here, i.e., an open and sober *dialogue* between faith and all levels of publicness. This dialogue must include critical aspects. Yet, its key aim should always be to contribute constructively to the building of our society and not to dictate it. As opposed to both exotic religious tourism and aggressive faith-based fundamentalism, the dialogue option would promote something we really need — namely, the presence of sound and sane expressions of publicly visible religion.

I shall not venture into an assessment of so-called postmodernism in this connection — a mixed and somewhat confusing phenomenon, not least when it is investigated within a broad cultural context. However, I seriously doubt that the postmodern, rather unreal approach to religion is capable of providing a proper framework for our dialogue with the public sphere at large. Actually, several of the problematic features and trends I have referred to above may be seen as more or less direct offspring of the present current. This is partly the case with the striking boost of popular culture, but most notably in view of a deconstruction of religion that points towards its aestheticization, privatization, and a disturbing loss of reality sense. Hence, our religious market can to a significant degree be seen as a postmodern thing.

Postmodernity has often been interpreted as expressing a new and more positive attitude towards religion as compared to modernism. This, however, is primarily due to its nearly unrestricted pluralism and a corresponding openness to just about anything. And it lies behind our interest in religious *curiosa* as well as the efforts to turn us into perpetual tourists within the sphere of religion. For postmodernity everything may appear to be equally valid, regardless of its sustainability and its anchoring in reality. There is thus no need for a rationally based critique or differentiation here.

Personally, I am not at all convinced that postmodernism is a better dialogue partner for the churches than modernism. Admittedly, various types of modernism reflect a certain skepticism or antagonism towards religion. At the same time, most modernist currents are committed to truths that are mutually binding and obligatory to all. They further maintain that truth must be coupled with reality. In many cases, such commitment may seem to be lacking within postmodernity. Seen from this perspective, the claimed religious openness of postmodernism can easily turn out to be a Pyrrhic victory for the churches. Let me here add that there is a need to reevaluate our relationship to modernity, as a corrective over against the recent propensity to revert to premodern attitudes.

In concluding this initial chapter, I would like to reiterate that I am aware that my account of present societal, cultural, and religious developments may come across as quite harsh and bleak. Yet, the inclination to immunize ourselves over against critical correctives must be rejected as clearly counterproductive. And realism is indispensable, particularly when it is experienced as uncomfortable — not least in identifying a viable strategy for the church's mission.

At any rate, these deliberations form a significant part of the background of my proposal of a "materialist spirituality." Such spirituality should be perceived as a critical spirituality, in the sense that it represents a corrective over against the dominating forces of the religious market. What is at stake here is a piety for our factual lives and for the world we live in.

Literature

Ali, Tariq. *The Clash of Fundamentalisms: Crusades, Jihads, and Modernity*. London: Verso, 2002.

Carrette, Jeremy, and Richard King. *Selling Spirituality: The Silent Takeover of Religion*. London: Routledge, 2005.

Chomsky, Noam. *The Prosperous Few and the Restless Many*. London: Pluto Press, 2003.

Erd, Rainer, Dietrich Hoss, Otto Jacobi, and Peter Noller, Hrsg. *Kritische Theorie und Kultur*. Frankfurt am Main: Suhrkamp, 1989.

Frank, Thomas. *One Market Under God: Extreme Capitalism, Market Populism, and the End of Economic Democracy*. New York: Random House, 2001.

Horkheimer, Max, and Theodor W. Adorno. *Dialectics of Enlightenment: Philosophical Fragments*. Palo Alto, CA: Stanford University Press, 2002. See especially the intriguing and highly prophetic essay on "The Culture Industry."

Jameson, Fredric. *Postmodernism: Or the Cultural Logic of Late Capitalism*. Durham, NC: Duke University Press, 1992.

Lyon, David. *Jesus in Disneyland: Religion in Postmodern Times*. Cambridge: Polity Press, 2000.

Martin, William. *With God on Our Side: The Rise of the Religious Right in America*, new edition. New York: Broadway Books, 2005.

Tracy, David. *The Spirituality Revolution: The Emergence of Contemporary Spirituality*. Oxford: Routledge, 2004.

2 Materialist Spirituality

What in the World . . . ? An Initial Definition

Allow me to start with some personal remarks: I was brought up within a typically Western Norwegian, neo-pietistically inclined and fairly low-church Lutheran piety and stayed there throughout the years of my youth. The key concern here was to have Jesus in your heart. This was combined with regular reading of the Bible, personal prayer, and a set of firm, if not too severe moral convictions. I am still grateful to those who introduced me to these practices, just as I continue to be struck by bad conscience if I miss out on the daily Scripture readings. Most importantly, it would be obtuse to question the benefit of having Jesus in one's heart. Yet, I must admit that this kind of piety worked more and more poorly in my case. Not because there was something wrong with the system as such, but rather because it became increasingly difficult to integrate it into my actual life. And a piety that can hardly be lived out is of little value.

My life was marked by buckets of stress, toil, and unrest — just as it is with most people today. It allowed minimal space for personal spiritual exercises. The intervals when I was supposed to be "alone with Jesus" became more and more cramped. The required spiritual concentration was at best feeble, at worst bordering on pure self-conceit. Even if I had a blood pump that worked more heavily than it should, I hardly had a "heart" where space could be provided for Jesus. This led to a longing for a spirituality that could be more effectively incorporated in my life; a piety that did not depend on my own — clearly insufficient — spiritual presence; something I could bring with me at work, in fellowship with family and friends, and during evening strolls — without presupposing a devoutness that I was unable to mobilize; an entity that was just there, independent of my efforts — just like grace in Christ; more on the line of the Orthodox "Jesus prayer" — being integrated in the breathing reflex.

For quite a while, I put my stakes in the worship life of the church — positioning myself as a "high-church" Lutheran. But I have to say that this too became increasingly difficult, especially since I at that time was living on the European continent and worshiping in a congregation with a strong Protestant identity. On the European scene, at least, high-church Lutheranism has become conspicuously marginalized during the last decades. Anyway, because of what I saw as a tiresome messing with the authentic liturgical structure of the service and the fact that — due to the way the sacrament was administered — the real presence was becoming more and more invisible, the whole project grew cumbersome to me. Eventually, I felt rather homeless in the church that was supposed to be my home on earth. Parallel to this, my search for a viable spirituality was coupled with a yearning to live a full sacramental life. To make a long story short: It was this that brought me to the Roman Catholic Church. Along similar lines, the personal process that prompted me towards a materialist spirituality can be described. Even if I insist that this kind of spirituality is ecumenically grounded and valid, my admittance into the full fellowship of the Catholic Church in January 2003 and the subsequent growing acquaintance with the rich sacramental life of the Catholic tradition were crucial in this connection.

I have often been asked what was so appealing to me in Catholic spirituality. Obviously, such spirituality is a very diverse phenomenon. In my case, clearly the most important thing was the emphasis on sacramentality, which opened up the possibility of living a full, sacramental life — and particularly to be able to take the Eucharist without wondering what I was being offered through the elements. In addition to this, the following factors played a vital role: First, the reassurance that our life in Christ is attached to outward signs and elementary sensation. In the Mass we sense and experience, rise and kneel, bow and make the sign of the cross. And we insist that none of these simple acts are random, but crucial in our spiritual life. As a Catholic priest once said to me when I somewhat reluctantly had to admit that I found it hard to concentrate in prayer: Seeing can be praying, too. Second, there is a conviction that God in the Mass deals with us mainly as a collective or as *communio* — and not as the sum of secluded individuals. I discovered the blessing of doing things together — if not with military precision, then at least with a certain amount of coordination. This corresponds to the conviction of the Old Church that a single Christian hardly is or can be a Christian, *unus christianus nullus christianus est*. Third, there was an openness to combining spirituality with plain rationality — presupposing that faith and reason should be considered complementary roads to God.

None of these concerns are in any way contrary to authentic Reformation identity. To me, however, they often seemed to be vanishing in an ocean of what I label as liberal-pietism. This is a different story. But I have elsewhere argued that the main problem with contemporary Lutheranism is that in my view it has departed significantly from the original message of the Reformers, largely coming across as a nineteenth-century phenomenon. It may seem odd, but I have had the experience that it is somehow easier to live out true Reformation identity within the Roman Catholic Church in its post–Vatican II shape.

"Materialist spirituality" — as already indicated, I am aware that this expression may sound paradoxical bordering on senselessness. In most cases, spirituality and materialism are understood as contradictory or even mutually excluding concepts. I have to admit that I have chosen the term partly in order to provoke. Now, being provocative is no goal in itself. But in a situation where spirituality has been turned into a vague and foggy commodity and where God's creation is seriously wounded, a materialist spirituality is bound to be provoking. And despite the paradoxical nature of the concept, it should not be dismissed as a futile game with words. In my view, such spirituality actualizes theological concerns of great significance. Before I move on to a basic definition, however, let me briefly underline what this is *not* about: Materialist spirituality is not an attempt to sketch a piety grounded in a materialist ideology. As much as I appreciate parts of Marxism and find it strange that this approach to society is considered outdated in the age of wild neo-liberalism and capitalist globalization, our life in Christ must be anchored elsewhere. This is even more so in regard to the massive "practical materialism" that is propagated through our increasingly consumerist culture.

What is it, then? In my efforts to define materialist spirituality, I start with an observation that stems from St. Benedict: The intention of liturgical chant is that our mind shall become conformed or equally shaped with our voices — *ut mens nostra concordet voci nostrae*. The act of singing, an engaging of the voice, is the forming principle, while the mind is being shaped — not the other way round. As far as I can gather, this simply implies that the outward form carries the inner spiritual meaning. Within some types of Protestantism, the opposite appears to be the case — desperately trying to squeeze a measure of "spirit" into forms that at the end of the day one does not really believe in and considering "outward religion" to be inferior. Such attitudes have set their mark on pietism as well as parts of liberal theology. And they can be retrieved in the proclivity towards abstraction that marks a significant part of contemporary Protestant thought. As opposed to this trend, a materialist spirituality insists that outward forms or shapes are fully capable of incorporating, conveying, and expressing inner spiritual substance.

On this basis, three central features of this kind of piety can be identified: What is at stake here is, first, a spirituality that is bound to concrete *materia* or stuff, primarily the holy sacraments and the sacramental dimension of Christian life in general. Materialist spirituality is above all a sacramentally founded spirituality. This points towards the Western-Augustinian teaching on sacramentality: A sacrament consists of a promise, *res* — more precisely, God's unwavering promise in Christ — and a tangible sign, *signum*. On the one hand, the promise or the thing itself is always theologically prior to the sign. On the other hand, the promise is fulfilled through and in connection with the sign. This means that the benefits of baptism are only accessible through water, and that the gifts of the Eucharist can be received solely through the elementary substances of bread and wine. In spite of their ordinary appearance, the sacraments are fully capable of delivering what they pledge: Through baptism we share in the death and resurrection of Christ (cf. Rom. 6), and in the Eucharist we truly become his body by eating and drinking (cf. 1 Cor. 12).

Subsequent to this, it must be underlined that materialist spirituality is not lived out in a spiritualized vacuum, but requires concrete spaces — namely the church and the world. Such piety is born within the church, but must always be lived out in and for the world — or

God's world. Even if these spaces are not identical, they are clearly interconnected. For the goal of the church and its service is not just the saving of a number of souls, but the redemption of God's creation: ". . . the creation itself will be set free from its bondage to decay and obtain the glorious liberty of the children of God" (Rom. 8:21). The church is the mother of faith and place of salvation. But it is also priest of creation and the first-fruit of a reunited humankind. It has been said that this dynamic interaction between church and world implies that when a single human being is lifted one tiny millimeter closer to God, the whole world will follow suit.

Third, materialist spirituality is not grounded in abstract and airy ideas, but in elementary and concrete empirical perception — i.e., in things we hear and see, smell and taste. Not least of the latter, in our celebration of the Eucharist. This corresponds to a crucial feature in the apostolic witness to Christ. The core of this witness is not sophisticated or spiritualized interpretation, but what the disciples actually had experienced in their life with Jesus: "That which . . . we have seen with our eyes, which we have looked upon and *touched with our hands,* concerning the word of life . . ." (1 John 1:1). A vital sacramental dimension is added to this in the story of the disciples' meeting with Jesus on the way to Emmaus: "When he was at the table with them, he took the bread and blessed, and broke it, and gave it to them. And their eyes were opened and they recognized him . . ." (Luke 24:30-31). Surely this is what happens in the Eucharist.

At the bottom of these features are a number of theological convictions of essential importance. I shall here have to settle with mentioning three of them:

1. The incarnation — or the fact that God's Son became a human being like us in everything, though without sin — means that there is no place where we can come, including the most despairing and desolate depths of life, without Jesus' having been there before us and remaining with us. It further entails an affirmation of all true humanity. This prompts us towards the exhortation of Philippians 4:8: ". . . whatever is true, whatever is honorable, whatever is just, whatever is pure, whatever is lovely, whatever is gracious, if there is any excellence, if there is anything worthy of praise, think about these things." Or to express it through the words of a newspaper headline: *Do as God, become human!* Accordingly, the incarnation functions as a corrective over against a

spirituality that ignores or even oppresses true humanity. It is, therefore, a chief paradigm of the church's life and service.

2. As indicated above, creation and redemption should not be mixed together, but definitely also not torn completely apart. Here we are looking at two sides of the same coin, and the key concern is simply to keep together what belongs together in God's plan of salvation. Through Christ it is God's aim and will to "reconcile to himself all things, whether on earth or in heaven, making peace by the blood of his cross" (Col. 1:20). The saving of human beings or of our "souls" is an integral part of this grand scheme for the redemption of creation. From creation we can draw lines to the sacraments and their signs, being taken more or less directly from the created world. It is vital to escape from the Gnostic tendencies and the neglect of creation that mark much contemporary theology, let alone the main strands of market spirituality. Here a materialist spirituality exercises yet another important critical function.

3. At the core of spirituality is our life in the Holy Spirit. It must, however, be stressed that pneumatology should not be treated as if it were a subdivision for theological curiosities. Quite on the contrary, the Spirit serves as the grounded wire of our Christian existence until Christ returns. This is reflected in Paul's practical and down-to-earth account of the fruits of the Spirit in Galatians 5:16-26. These are ". . . love, joy, peace, patience, kindness, goodness, faithfulness, gentleness, self-control" — i.e., not specifically religious deeds, but crucial virtues in human life. Similarly, "the works of the flesh" that put our spiritual life at jeopardy include "ecumenical" impediments or barriers to human unity — such as "enmity, strife, jealousy, anger, selfishness, dissension, party spirit, envy." Obviously, this does not mean that the more extraordinary, charismatic gifts are insignificant. But these things must be properly balanced. In the wake of this, it should be noted that John's Gospel is the one that deals most thoroughly with the Spirit. Yet it contains no direct reference to the special charismatic gifts — suggesting that the work of the Holy Spirit must not be confused with its extraordinary effects.

Along these lines, the full Trinitarian anchoring of materialist spirituality is manifested and affirmed. A viable Christian piety must reflect these essential facts: God is the creator; he has created the world and never leaves it. Christ is the redeemer; he saves us and redeems

creation through his reconciling offering at the cross. The Holy Spirit is
the giver of life, adding dynamism and vitality to our existence through
outward signs and in the concrete space of the church. Here the key intention is to secure the correct balance between the three divine persons. The chief problem with a vast number of heresies is that they
have failed in accounting for this balance. Christomonism may look deceptively pious, but it is nonetheless theologically inadequate and counterproductive.

I shall elaborate the just-noted essential theological concerns further in
the next chapters — while hoping to avoid too much repetition. The
point at this stage has simply been to register these concerns as foundational principles of a materialist spirituality. Before I conclude this attempt to provide an initial definition, however, some significant practical aspects of this type of piety must be underscored through five brief
theses:

- Materialist spirituality can be perceived as a "democratic" spirituality in the sense that it is accessible to all human beings through
  basic empirical perception and does not presuppose a special religious "antenna system."
- Materialist spirituality emerges as straightforward and simple by
  being grounded in the reassuring fact that God comes to us
  through elementary earthly things — e.g., water, wine, and bread.
  Having been exposed to noisier types of piety, I am tempted to
  exclaim: God be praised for dullness!
- In focusing on our daily life and stressing our responsibility to cultivate creation for God's honor and the benefit of all our neighbors, materialist spirituality comes across as positively earthbound
  or "worldly."
- Materialist spirituality is a spirituality of fellowship and concrete
  solidarity, meaning that it is lived out in and for the community.
  Hence, it also provides space for the rich complementarities of
  women and men.
- The liturgy and the additional sign language of the church play a
  key role within the framework of a materialist spirituality. Here it
  must be noted that this sign language should not be exposed to
  hazy abstraction, excessive intricacy, or false spiritualism. The

present language is in many respects just as downright and uncomplicated as any human language and speaks to us primarily as human beings: We wash when we have become unclean, we eat when we are hungry, the laying on of hands must be understood in analogy with a human expression of friendship and love, etc.

All in all, materialist spirituality emerges as a piety that smells freshly of earth and at the same time conveys a solid taste of heaven. It assumes that there can be no true spirituality without a proper relationship to the world. And it can be characterized as a "spirituality from below" in the sense that it is communicated to us through our lives and basic human experience (Anselm Grün). At the same time, it refrains from ignoring the vertical origins of our life in Christ. More specifically, this kind of spirituality is inspired by *inter alia* Catholic sacramentality and Lutheran vocation ethics. While the first of these approaches in some cases may need a reminder on the basic earthliness of sacramentality, the second would benefit from an explicit sacramental foundation. Within these frames, materialist spirituality seeks to hold together things that are often considered opposites and thus torn apart, but still clearly belong together in Christian life.

Materialist spirituality is further marked by solidarity, care, and compassion. This is anchored in the example of Jesus: "For you know the grace of our Lord Jesus Christ, that though he was rich, yet for your sake he became poor, so that by his poverty you might become rich" (2 Cor. 8:9). Seen from our perspective, it can be expressed as follows: ". . . above all these put on love, which binds everything together in perfect harmony" (Col. 3:14). Here the diaconal ministry of the church and the mission of the faithful in its entirety are actualized. A materialist piety thus aims at escaping from the propensity for self-centered, feel-good religiosity and the stripping of religion of its moral contents that characterize much contemporary market spirituality.

Moreover, materialist spirituality deviates from all falsely spiritualized and biased "heavenly" theologies. Such concepts are in effect bound to promote secularization. Surely, there is a secularization that emerges as both legitimate and necessary. For the world must be treated as sovereign and mature in regard to its integral wisdom, as well as its belonging to God's creation. It cannot, therefore, be governed by theocratic measures. However, secularization becomes illegitimate if it tears God and world apart. Somewhat paradoxically, radical spiritualism and radical immanentism here draw in the same direction.

Yet, it must be acknowledged that one-sidedly earthbound theologies have been inclined to ignore or forget the church. As the mother of faith and the place of salvation, the church plays an essential and indispensable role in a materialist spirituality — in accordance with the assertion of St. Cyprian that we cannot have God as father unless we have the church as mother. Faith is born in the church mainly through the water of baptism, it is nourished by its rich sacramental life, and it is sustained by the unfailing encounter with Christ that is at the core of its nature and mission. However, this church cannot be separated from the world. It is also the priest of creation and the first-fruit of a reunited humankind. And it is an efficient or sacramental sign of God's kingdom. In the Gospels, this kingdom is described as an entity where the last come in first, the smallest are the greatest, and children have the priority. This is unlike the world we have deplorably produced, but totally in keeping with God's will for his creation — serving as a forceful critical corrective. Along these lines, a materialist spirituality aims at keeping together the vertical and the horizontal dimensions of church life.

In sum, materialist spirituality is palpable and down-to-earth, elementary and immediate, vertically directed and horizontally anchored. As compared to the most colorful and exotic options laid out for sale in today's religious marketplace, my bid for a viable spirituality will probably come across as trivial and unexciting. However, when life gets complicated, the concrete and solid are often far more helpful than market-sensitive flamboyance. In an age of postmodern volatility or flimsiness and of a "reality-TV" that takes us way beyond any conceivable form of reality, there is a clear need for sound realist practicality — also among God's people. Materialist spirituality invites us to a highly required revisiting of reality.

Having identified the basic meaning and central implications of a materialist spirituality, I now turn to some brief remarks on its roots. I have not come across this expression elsewhere. However, its fundamental intention and idea seem to have several equivalents. Olivier Clement somewhere talks about "mystical materialism." The Eucharistic theology of Alexander Schmemann points in a similar direction. William

Temple depicted Christianity as the most "materialist" of all religions, in a positive sense. Both the Ignatian tradition and current Ignatian-based methods stress that personal spiritual experience is grounded in things that are available to all, and thus functions as a door to reality. Karl Rahner suggests that we are led from creation to the Creator and then back again to creation, alluding to the concept *sacramentum mundi*. While some types of feminist theology differ from our concept, others are comparable — especially so with feminist contributions to liturgical theology. And the Marxist culture critic Walter Benjamin (1892-1940) even talked about a "materialist theology."

When we look back at history, antecedents of a materialist spirituality can be found there too — though of a more implicit kind. Through some of my references here, I hope I have already been able to indicate that such piety is in keeping with Holy Scripture. Further scriptural evidence will be given in the subsequent account. Classic Christian spirituality abstained from the lure of vagueness and elusiveness, in its Gnostic as well as its overly enthusiastic shapes. Quite to the contrary, this piety was directed towards something highly palpable — namely our life in the Spirit in God's world. This concurs with the insistence that "the tree is known by its fruit" (Matt. 12:33), and not by its lofty ideas.

Similar concerns marked the spirituality that grew forth within the Old Church, in a cultural context that in many respects resembles our situation today. This was especially the case as Christianity became the leading religion within the Roman Empire. Desert fathers, radical ascetics, and early monastery life may appear to point in a different direction. But these forms of piety were also anchored in the world; enduring and committed prayer for humankind played a key role. Moreover, asceticism and solidarity with those in need were often held together. Even the most contemplative and introspective forms of spirituality were somehow connected with the church's mission in the world.

From these currents there are more or less direct lines to the Reformation. This is affirmed by its focus on the theology of creation. However, Lutheran vocation ethics point in the same direction — presupposing that we encounter God's will for our lives in basic human and social relations. Other, more recent examples can be found in the activity of the first missionary societies — with their efforts to hold evangelization and charity together; in the modern ecumenical movement — which developed these concerns further; and in the statements of the Second Vatican Council — correcting anti-modernist attitudes and emphasizing the sending of the church to the modern world.

Generally, materialist spirituality aims at drawing from the abundantly rich sources of tradition. Seen in this perspective, it presupposes that there is no need for the church to venture into the tiresome and unproductive business of reinventing the wheel. And it takes note of John Cardinal Newman's pertinent admonition against anything that may lead to a loss of a basic sense of history. At the same time, our joy in tradition must never be allowed to develop in the direction of the dead-end of nostalgicism. This is a danger within parts of Roman Catholicism today, with their inclination towards premodern sentiments and their disregard of the essential contents and implications of Vatican II. Accordingly, it must be underlined that the immense constructive potential of tradition requires that it is unfolded within the indispensable framework of present realities. This compares to the insistence of St. Bernard that the church has been equipped with eyes to look backward as well as forward. I shall return to the relevance of modernity and modernism at this point later on.

In exploring a materialist spirituality further, there are several ditches that must be avoided. Some may find my account so far to be biased or incomplete, in the sense that the earthbound nature, elementary immediacy, and basic plainness of Christian life have been stressed too forcefully. This depends on my wish to elucidate the critical dimension of the concept as a corrective over against shallow market spiritualities outside as well as inside the church — calling for a distinction between "spirituality" and "spiritualism." As already pointed out, I seriously doubt that the longing for a viable, sustainable, and functioning piety can be filled by charismatic showiness or well-polished prophets of prosperity, by private religion or spiritual nostalgia, by popular mysticism or monastic tourism. Today's religious situation reflects a demand for a spirituality capable of functioning where it shall and must function — namely in our daily existence and amidst current realities. And as opposed to the feel-good industry, we need a piety that can be a bit cumbersome in our lives.

Yet, it must be admitted that a one-sidedly "secularized" spirituality is also incapable of providing a solution to this challenge. The essential vertical anchoring of Christian faith cannot and should not be neglected. Let me therefore underscore that I am not blind to the fact that a careful balance is required in this area. I believe it was Blaise Pascal who suggested that there are two serious errors here: The first one is to take everything literally, the second one is to take everything spiritually. We have to find our way between these two extremes.

In the wake of this, there are many factors that must be balanced: creation and redemption, the world and the church, the vertical and the horizontal dimensions of Christian life, reason and revelation, works and faith, ethics and evangelization, etc. The relationship between the invisible nature of our hope in Christ and its visible manifestations requires special attention in our context. Paul states that "we walk by faith, not by sight" (2 Cor. 5:7). He also maintains, however, that " 'What no eye has seen, nor ear heard, nor the heart of man conceived, what God has prepared for those who love him,' God has revealed to us through the Spirit. For the Spirit searches everything, even the depths of God" (1 Cor. 2:9-10). Thus seen, the first of these statements is primarily directed against the pursuit of shimmering spiritualized experiences. This is in line with Martin Luther's insistence that it is the impious who crave such experiences — *impii experiri volunt*, while the truly pious settle for the invisible. Still, this does not exclude a basic perceptibility. I shall return to this later on, particularly in my discussion of the importance of art.

My main concern at this point is that the just-mentioned diverging concepts and the question of the proper balance between them should be assessed in conjunction with an open and dynamic both-and approach — not within the framework of a cramped and static either-or perspective. Seen in light of the abundance of the church's faith deposit, minimalist and reductionist attitudes must be rejected as counterproductive. And surely, materialist spirituality aims at our becoming richer in faith — not poorer. This corresponds with the concept of catholicity. Even if this concept cannot be flatly identified with "comprehensiveness," the Catholic project definitely calls for a substantial amount of human generosity — as well as the gradually vanishing ability to keep two thoughts in our mind at the same time.

In the end, the key intention of a materialist spirituality is to affirm and express *the corporeality of Christian faith in its concrete embodiment in our life in the church and the world.* "Corporeal" is a highly appropriate term in this connection, reflecting both the body-dimension of faith and its anchoring in reality. These concerns are essential to our theology as well as our piety.

A fine and impressive account of central aspects of such spirituality — with special focus on its ecclesial and sacramental dimensions — can be found in one of the novels of Sigrid Undset, the Norwegian writer who converted to the Roman Catholic Church and became a Nobel laureate in literature. Here I am thinking of some paragraphs from *Gymnadenia* (1929) — or *The Wild Orchid*, as the English translation is titled — which describe the key figure Paul Selmer's first visit in St. Olav's Catholic Church in Oslo. I quote extracts from the section:

> The body of the church was filled with shadows, and now and again it seemed vast and lofty, but home-like all the same — all the mass of things they had on the altars and round about showed but vaguely and gave the impression that the church was a place where people lived day by day. [. . .] And high up in the darkness of the choir hung a little red lamp with a flickering flame within it.
>
> There was no one in the church. Paul walked softly up the centre of the nave and entered the pew. With some hesitation he put down his hat, pulled up his trousers and knelt down. He hid his face in his hands. . . . [. . .]
>
> How does one address God? I've never tried to talk to him before. — Our Father which art in heaven — so one says *thou* to God. He gave a little embarrassed laugh behind his hands. It was so odd, his kneeling here in Saint Olav's church to pray to God.
>
> He tried to think why it was exactly that he had landed here, peeped up and fixed his eyes on the little flickering red flame in the darkness. And all at once it dawned on him, so that he felt shaken all over — if what that little red lamp hung there to proclaim was true — why then, why then!
>
> If *that* was the truth about Jesus — of whom he had heard so much talk, humanly discursive, humanly cock-sure talk, that he was utterly sick of the very name — if *that* was the truth, that here He was actually present in a mysterious way, confined in something material, a sacrament — and somewhere in the lower depths of his being Paul had a sudden knowledge of what a sacrament was, though he understood nothing of it. If it was true that He was *here*, present in this

way and at the same time on thousands and thousands of other altars
— then He must also be present in another way everywhere and at all
times, an eye that embraced the beginning of the spheres in space and
the interior of the atoms and the secret thoughts of men in one single
glance without distinction between past and present, great and small
— everything was merely His thought and everything contemporary
and everything equally clear and dear.

He felt the skin of his face grow cold and stiff, while his heart
was like a burning heat in his breast. If this was the truth, then the
whole of life was inconceivably more wonderful and dangerous and
rich, so unspeakably more serious and valuable than he had ever
dreamt. He had a glimpse of paths which led out into a darkness beyond his imagining, and forward into a light that he scarcely dared
to divine.

It is simply too good to be true.

He crouched still lower with his face buried in his hands.

It was as though he *saw* — concentrated in one point — that this
was not impossible of belief. Truth might be just as fantastic as this.
But he felt himself shrink up with dread at the thought that this
truth was to enter into his life, as though facing a terrible effort. I
am the Truth, Jesus had said. It had never occurred to him before to
consider at all closely what those words really implied. Though he
had had a vague presentiment that the Truth was something he did
not know, and that all he knew was a kind of unreality. Although no
doubt it *was* reality in a way; all that was lacking was the explanation of what this reality might be good for. Just as an unlighted lamp
is real, but a savage who has never seen it burning cannot guess what
its use may be.

— So I suppose I've got to try and find out how one sets about
praying.

He looked up towards the choir — again he felt a kind of shiver:
is He there really, shut up in a little box in the dark? Voluntarily —
He at whose will worlds come into being and are dissolved — ?
Waiting, waiting, for the half-dozen people who come here every
morning, for the congregation that fills the church on Sundays, for
the solitary creature who turns in from the street to speak with the
One and Only.

God's patience — the thought struck Paul as the central point of

all this — that what we call patience is but a little image of something inconceivable — God's patience.

"Jesus, Jesus, be patient with me too."

He would have to attempt the Lord's Prayer anyhow — try if he
knew it.

Paul straightened himself on his knees. Before he was conscious
of it he had made the sign of the cross, as he had seen the Gotaas's
do at the table.

"Our Father, which art in heaven, hallowed be thy Name. Thy
kingdom come. Thy will be done in earth, as it is in heaven" —
when he had finished he had not thought of a single one of the
words he uttered, merely felt happy to find he still knew it all by
heart.

But then — ? To pray *for* something seemed so cheap. The very
moment he had begun to think of it as a possibility that men might
achieve contact with God, he could not very well come forward
with requests.

He remained kneeling against the back of the bench in front,
with his arms crossed on his breast, feeling nothing but the darkness
and the stillness and the little red light high up which seemed satu-
rated with something real and good.

[. . .]

Then three nuns appeared in the lighted choir. [. . .] Paul observed their movements with attention, trying to make out what
the ceremony might be intended to express: probably it was in
some way symbolical of confession. Till one of the nuns suddenly
produced a big feather brush and started dusting the paper flowers
in a vase. — Oh, that was it; they were charwomen. — He felt kind
of foolish. Presently he went out. (*The Wild Orchid*, pp. 225-29)

Finally, Mary — the mother of God and our mother — stands forth as
yet another important icon of materialist spirituality. Simultaneously,
she reflects the positively practical and down-to-earth nature of much
female religiosity. In the text on the annunciation (cf. Luke 1:26-38), a
certain tension may be spotted between the overwhelming and somewhat affected message of the angel and the obedient, but also blunt and
matter-of-fact response of the young teenage girl: How on earth can
this happen, I have never been together with a man?

Seen against this background, Mary can be depicted as Our Lady of Holy Earthliness. Not in the sense of yet another expression of "female humility," but as a model of an attentive mind and a readiness to serve. Mary simply notes what is required of her — and does it, without large gestures, and with confidence in God.

Confronted with this, we exclaim: Glory to God in the highest, he who reigns over the cherubs. But we are quick to add: Glory to God in the lowest, he who has "regarded the low state of his handmaiden" and never abandons the heavily burdened. Both these affirmations are crucial to materialist spirituality.

Literature

Barton, Stephen C. *The Spirituality of the Gospels.* Eugene, OR: Wipf & Stock, 2006.

Bonhoeffer, Dietrich. *The Cost of Discipleship.* London: SCM Press, 2001.

Clement, Olivier. *Sources: Les Mystiques Chrétiens des Origines.* Paris: Éditions Stock, 1999.

Greeley, Andrew. *The Catholic Imagination.* Berkeley: University of California Press, 2000.

Jones, Cheslyn, Geoffrey Wainwright, and Edward Yarnold, eds. *The Study of Spirituality.* London: SPCK, 1986.

Murphy, Francesca Aran. *God Is Not a Story: Realism Revisited.* New York: Oxford University Press, 2007.

Reno, R. R. *The Ordinary Transformed: Karl Rahner and the Christian Vision of Transcendence.* Grand Rapids: Eerdmans, 1995.

Schmemann, Alexander. *For the Life of the World: Sacraments and Orthodoxy.* Crestwood, NY: St. Vladimir's Seminary Press, 1989.

Sheldrake, Philip. *A Brief History of Spirituality.* Oxford: Blackwell, 2007.

Tracy, David. *The Analogical Imagination: Christian Theology and the Culture of Pluralism.* New York: Crossroads, 1982.

Undset, Sigrid. *The Wild Orchid.* Translated from the Norwegian by Arthur G. Chater. New York: Alfred A. Knopf, 1941.

TRINITARIAN FOUNDATION

3 Creation and Redemption

Two Sides of the Same Coin

God's work as creator and redeemer has often been torn apart in a rather violent manner. A recurring consequence of this misapprehension is that we become so fixed on our own personal salvation that we ignore our connectedness with and responsibility for the created world. This often comes across as a form of spiritual egoism, an obsession with religious feel-good sentiments — or perhaps as a Christian accommodation to a neo-conservative or wildly liberalist ideology. There are, however, also examples of the opposite extreme. This is the case when creation becomes dominating in a biased or secluded way — forgetting that the created world cannot save itself, but needs redemption in Christ. Such an attitude can be found in some versions of so-called political theology. A more implicit, but in effect far worse example, is the proclivity towards "practical materialism" that keeps invading us as Christians, too.

A materialist spirituality is committed to holding these two sides of God's mission together — not just at the level of abstract ideas, but also in our concrete practice. This pertains to the three persons of the Trinity, all participating in the act of creation: The Father is the creator, the Son is the ultimate liberator of creation, and the Holy Spirit conveys life to all created beings. Surely, a misplaced confusion of creation and redemption must be avoided. Yet, these aspects should never be divided by tight fences. In God's plan of salvation they clearly belong together, as two sides of the same coin. And what unites them is primarily the incarnation, the fact that the Son of God became flesh like us.

Christ embodies the affirmation of God's unwavering *yes* to the world and humanity. As a boundless act of solidarity, the incarnation and its vital implications in regard to the interconnection between creation and redemption contribute significantly to the foundation of a materialist spirituality. Our life in Christ must also reflect this fact. Subsequently, the sacraments and sacramentality are also essential in keeping creation and redemption together. The sacramental acts are efficient expressions of God's grace in Christ, being communicated to us through signs or elements from the created world.

Several currents have failed in keeping creation and redemption together — or in securing a proper balance between these two interrelated sides of God's work. Late pietism or neo-pietism ended up in this ditch, advocating a strongly personalized perception of salvation at the cost of creation theology. The spiritual proxy of these currents, a deistically inclined romanticism, pointed towards the opposite extreme. Here it was fervently argued that God and nature were identical entities. This implied that creation carries its own salvation within itself, having no need for an external savior. Such sentiments were crucial to the romantic "artist religion" of the nineteenth century. While today's neo-charismatics largely follow in the footsteps of late pietism, neo-religious market spiritualities are more unpredictable. Parts of this movement opt for privatized "feel-goodism"; other parts tend to deify nature.

Yet, these opposing positions have one thing in common: They react critically towards "institutionalized religion." Accordingly, they come across as ecclesiologically counterproductive in the sense that they minimize or even completely neglect the church's role in the drama of salvation. A possible example of such a view can be found in a small early poem by Emily Dickinson:

> Some keep the Sabbath going to church;
> I keep it staying at home,
> With a bobolink for a chorister,
> And an orchard for a dome.
>
> Some keep the Sabbath in surplice;
> I just wear my wings,
> And instead of tolling the bells for church,
> Our little sexton sings.

God preaches, — a noted clergyman —
And the sermon is never long;
So instead of getting to heaven at last,
I'm going all along!

(from The Collected Poems
of Emily Dickinson, pp. 110-11)

This suggests that our efforts to hold creation and redemption together are significant in the field of ecclesiology, too. If there is a bias here — in either direction, the church tends to disappear from the horizon. Seen in this perspective, two central concerns of a materialist spirituality emerge as interconnected: A proper balance between world and church — i.e., the two key spaces of such piety — requires a properly balanced perception of the relationship between creation and redemption. And this also applies the other way round.

The biblical account of the history of salvation is essential in regard to our efforts to describe the interconnection between creation and redemption: God created the world and "saw that it was good" (Gen. 1:25); then there was a tragic fall that led God's creation into a situation of oppression, injustice, and pain; Christ's coming to the world is the beginning of a process whose aim is that the suffering creation shall be redeemed. This depends on the fact that the creator never abandons his creation. The Bible is often read solely from the perspective of personal salvation. Yet, the above-registered features play a crucial role in the biblical story of the drama of salvation. For example:

> I consider that the sufferings of this present time are not worth comparing with the glory that is to be revealed to us. For the creation waits with eager longing for the revealing of the sons of God; for the creation was subjected to futility, not of its own will but by the will of him who subjected it in hope; because the creation itself will be set free from its bondage to decay and obtain the glorious liberty of the children of God. We know that the whole creation has been groaning in travail together until now; and not only the creation, but we ourselves, who have the first fruits of the Spirit, groan inwardly as we wait for adoption as sons, the redemption of our bodies. (Rom. 8:18-23)

He is the image of the invisible God, the first-born of all creation; for in him all things were created, in heaven and on earth, visible and invisible, whether thrones or dominions or principalities or authorities — all things were created through him and for him. He is before all things, and in him all things hold together. He is the head of the body, the church; he is the beginning, the first-born from the dead, that in everything he might be preeminent. For in him all the fullness of God was pleased to dwell, and through him to reconcile to himself all things, whether on earth or in heaven, making peace by the blood of his cross. (Col. 1:15-20)

Then I saw a new heaven and a new earth; for the first heaven and the first earth had passed away, and the sea was no more. And I saw the holy city, new Jerusalem, coming down out of heaven from God, prepared as a bride adorned for her husband; and I heard a loud voice from the throne saying, "Behold, the dwelling of God is with men. He will dwell with them, and they shall be his people, and God himself will be with them; he will wipe away every tear from their eyes, and death shall be no more, neither shall there be mourning nor crying nor pain any more, for the former things have passed away." And he who sat upon the throne said, "Behold, I make all things new." (Rev. 21:1-5)

These quotations substantiate what I have said about the interrelatedness of creation and redemption. Actually, without creation there is nothing to save — creation is the "stuff" of salvation. This points towards some essential concerns: First, creation and its destiny should be seen as the basic framework of our personal salvation — and not the other way round. Second, this actualizes the immense cosmic scope of Christ's redeeming work — not merely aiming at the saving of a certain number of souls. Third, the church is fully integrated in this pungent cosmic vision. Fourth, we are saved as bodies and not only as souls. And fifth, our Christian hope is directed towards the redemption of creation and a "new earth" where the fatal consequences of the fall are mended.

At the same time, it must be underlined that a fallen creation really needs to be redeemed — it even "groans in travail," waiting for this glorious event. The Danish theologian Regin Prenter depicts the crucial dialectics between creation and redemption along the following lines: Creation is the start of redemption, while redemption is the completion of creation. A more appropriate way of expressing this can hardly be found. It also directs us forward to the fulfillment of our hope in Christ. At the end of this process, even death — our ultimate enemy — shall be defeated or "swallowed up in victory" (1 Cor. 15:54).

In light of this, we get a glimpse of another relationship that is fundamental to both Christian faith in general and a materialist spirituality — namely the interconnection between world and church. For the church can be seen as "a redeemed piece of world" (Dietrich Bonhoeffer). This compares to my previous insistence that the church is the priest of creation and the first-fruit of a reunited humankind. The bonds between world and church are consequences of the interrelation between creation and redemption. These things belong closely together in God's plan of salvation. They must, therefore, also be kept just as closely together in our spiritual life. When the first Christians — being a tiny and insignificant minority in society — were able to maintain the immense cosmic scope of the drama of salvation in Christ, it becomes odd when we today are so bent on retracting into cramped, personalized, or private positions. This is yet another reminder that the proclivity to neglect creation in much contemporary theological reflection must be counteracted.

Let us, then, take a closer look at some central features of the theology of creation and its implications in connection with a materialist spirituality:

First, the Christian concept of creation implies that the world and everything that fills it have come into existence and continue to exist through God's compassionate act of creation. There is in my opinion no need to develop in too much detail how this may have occurred in more concrete terms. Obviously, the narrative of creation is marked by a worldview that is largely obsolete or outdated today. I thus have to admit that I am inclined to see so-called creationist approaches as unnecessary crutches — not least if they are coupled more or less directly with a disregard of the indispensable ethical and socio-political implications of God's work as creator. The key concern here is that the whole of creation and all created beings have God as their source or point of departure. This confidence is basic to a materialist spirituality.

Second, human beings are given a special place in the created world. In the biblical narrative of creation, this is expressed through the thought that we are images of God and, hence, his collaborators or helpers at the level of creation — exercising a form of leadership over other created beings. At the same time, it is important to stress that we are entirely dependent on creation as a whole in our life. Furthermore, the world God has created can never be reduced to the level of pure instrumentality, just as it cannot be perceived solely as an arena for human self-realization. Theological reflection has often been marked by a too-narrow focus on the human being, at the expense of the rest of creation. It is, therefore, vital to acknowledge that the theology of creation includes an all-embracing responsibility to contribute to a good, proper, and just stewardship of the created world in its totality. To everyone who is capable of seeing, environmental problems and the desperate need of a sustainable way of life emerge as key challenges today. Accordingly, ecological awareness and accountability are fundamental concerns within a materialist spirituality.

The notion of creation further implies that *all* human beings are images of God. This shows that the cynical grading of human life that has become ever more common and influential in our societies is contrary to the intention of our creator. All human beings are included in the limitless love and compassion of God. They are therefore also entitled to our affection and solidarity. This applies to every life — poor as well as rich, unborn as well as born, old as well as young. In accordance with God's good will, we have a special responsibility for the deprived, suffering, and oppressed: ". . . if any one has the world's goods and sees his brother in need, yet closes his heart against him, how does God's love abide in him?" (1 John 3:17). Hence, a materialist spirituality departs radically from our proclivity to adore the beautiful, prosperous, and hip — knowing that all human beings are immensely precious in the eyes of God. And it is committed to implementing this insight through concrete solidarity.

Third, the theology of creation affirms that God acts as creator also after the fall. In this connection, we talk about *creatio continua* — a continual creation. When God continues his work as creator, it does not take place through vague ideas or nice thoughts. It happens in a far more concrete manner — partly by providing his creation with what it needs to maintain its life, and partly through his will for creation. This will is frequently perceived as something horrifying, or as a kind of religious superego that reflects God's harsh and punishing sides. Now, this too can be seen as belonging to the full picture — meaning that God transcends shallow pleasantries. He fervently opposes everything that puts the world he has created at jeopardy. However, God's will or his law is first and foremost a gift — it actually ranks among the best gifts that can be conceived. This simply depends on the fact that he who is the creator always knows what is best for his creation. A more sound guidance for our lives and the life of the whole world cannot be found. In accordance with this, materialist spirituality holds that real self-realization and true humanity means standing in a proper relationship to our creator and his will.

Fourth, God's continual creation also takes place through what has been labeled as ordinances of creation. Here marriage and family life play key roles. Many consider the state and political authorities to be ordinances of creation, too. At this point, it must be noted that such institutions are basically capable of functioning as channels for God's good will for his creation. Yet, there is certainly nothing automatic about this. Some Lutheran theologians in Germany during the early stages of the Nazi regime argued that any given government should be understood and respected as a tool of God. Today, however, the demonic evilness of the Nazi regime as well as the sufferings that other states have inflicted upon people are more than evident. This shows that all ordinances of creation or worldly institutions require God's revealed and good will as a critical corrective. Seen against this background, a materialist spirituality is aware that political commitment, love in solidarity, and sustainable stewardship clearly belong to our responsibility as created in God's image.

Fifth, after the fall in the created world, sin and its devastating consequences appear as almost irresistible forces. This is the reason why God's good will in many situations may seem to falter or fail to achieve its aim. It further explains why we often are incapable of doing the right things we want to do — instead, doing the things we deplore (cf. Rom. 7:15). And it lies underneath the greatest enigma of all, e.g., the question of why wickedness exercises such a power over us both as individuals and in our world. Here we are confronted with the highly vexing issue referred to as "the problem of evil." In an effort to respond to these distressing questions, I only have some simple observations to offer: Even if we cannot escape from the influence of sin, this does not mean that the world's nature as God's creation is annulled or invalidated. Moreover, after the fall human beings live under the dominion of sin. But this is not the only thing that can be said about us. For we are not just sinners; we are also struck by and menaced by sin. And — most importantly — God never leaves us in our agony and despair. As a matter of fact, he is fully capable of working good things in and through sinful human beings. Materialist spirituality therefore aims at counteracting the *laissez-faire*-like resignation that the power of sin and the persistence of evil occasionally have led to. And it stresses that our duty is to fight against evil at all levels — within ourselves as well as in society, in our souls as well as in political structures.

In the wake of this, the question of the interrelation between God's grace and human nature is actualized. Here Thomas Aquinas reasoned as follows: Grace does not cancel our nature, but perfects it — *gratia non tollit naturam sed perfecit*. This does not mean that there is an equally leveled cooperation between nature and grace that makes it possible to "earn" salvation. The point is rather to avoid having humans reduced to heteronymous puppets, also in regard to our redemption. God's grace in Christ works for us — *pro nos* — as well as in us — *in nobis*. Grace is therefore also a gift and a liberating force that enables us to do good things in Christ. Or to put it differently: We are saved through grace, in accordance with the *sola gratia* principle. Yet, grace is never "alone"; it is accompanied by good works. According to this, materialist spirituality dares to believe that human beings, created by God, possess an ability to see what is right in light of God's good will, and are able to put it into practice, thanks to God's gracious equipping of us.

In concluding my embarrassingly brief account of the interconnection between creation and redemption, I shall focus on some crucial practical implications of this relationship. Here it should be reiterated that this concern cannot be reduced to the level of abstract theories, but requires concrete and practical implementation. At this stage, I have to restrict myself to the three concerns:

1. The notion of the world as sacrament is vital at this point. It shows that the interconnectedness of creation and redemption works in both directions. There is, therefore, no one-way traffic here that may promote a false sacralization or theologization of creation. Quite on the contrary, when the world is seen as sacrament, the key concern is that it

functions as a real and effective arena for our encounter with the Triune God in its own right. In more specific terms, the *sacramentum mundi* concept suggests that we are led from creation to the creator and then back again to creation. This reflects the dynamic potential of the present notion. My previous reference to a certain measure of secularization as a legitimate expression of the inherent "maturity" of the world points in the same direction. Simultaneously, it must be kept in mind that a more complete image of God can only be unfolded within the framework of the dialectic between creation and redemption. And the full picture will only be revealed to us when Christ's work has been fulfilled. Then "we all, with unveiled face, beholding the glory of the Lord, [will be] changed into his likeness from one degree to another . . ." (2 Cor. 3:18).

2. Along the same line, my intention in stressing the interconnection between creation and redemption is not to turn the world into an object of devotion, but rather to identify it as a sphere of concrete ethical commitment. Here the concept of solidarity — being strongly anchored in a Christian-humanistic tradition — plays a highly essential role. The fact that creation and redemption are held together in God's plan of salvation has crucial consequences for Christian ethics in general and for the relationship between faith and ethics in particular. Again, the key point is to keep together what belongs together in God's grand scheme for the whole created world. I shall return to this — and several other related issues — in the following chapters.

3. A full and true theology of creation requires environmental consciousness and an accountable ecological practice. Especially in facing the evident fact of global warming and its multiplying consequences — clearly ranking among the most important challenges for humanity today, such consciousness is absolutely mandatory. All attempts to ignore or refute what is happening here must be branded as violations of God's good will for his creation — thus having sinful implications. This is not about "political correctness"; it is about the destiny of our earth. Seen from this angle, our theology of creation must include a sound eco-theology. It must further be able to present a constructive vision of what it means to provide positive stewardship for the world. And it must force us to realize that the environmental challenges require personal action and changes towards a new and sustainable lifestyle. Once more, this calls for ethical commitment rather than deification of the earth.

As I have tried to indicate through these three points, there is in my view no need to turn the world into an object of devotion. I am aware that this lies close to the preferred option of huge parts of contemporary neo-religiosity, *inter alia* as reflected in some of the Gaia-myths. To me, however, the contrary approach seems more fitting — namely a stressing of the earthliness or earth-bound aspects of redemption. This does not mean that the indispensable vertical grounding and eschatological direction of our faith life are neglected. But there are only two interconnected spaces where this life can be lived out right now — namely, in the world and in the church that is the priest of creation. Heaven will have to wait. And after all, it would make little sense to theologize, sacralize, or deify the earth when God's only Son entered our world as a human being and became our brother. In the incarnation, the opposite direction is at the core.

Literature

Bequette, John P. *Christian Humanism: Creation, Redemption and Reintegration.* Lanham, MD: University Press of America, 2005.

Birch, Charles, William Eakin, and Jay Byrd McDaniel. *Liberating Life: Contemporary Approaches to Ecological Theology.* Eugene, OR: Wipf & Stock, 2007.

Boff, Leonardo. *Cry of the Earth — Cry of the Poor.* Maryknoll, NY: Orbis, 1997.

Bonhoeffer, Dietrich. *Creation and Fall: A Theological Exposition of Genesis 1–3.* Bonhoeffer Works, vol. 3. Minneapolis: Augsburg Fortress, 1998.

Dickinson, Emily. *The Collected Poems of Emily Dickinson,* new edition. New York: Barnes & Noble, 1993.

Fergusson, David. *The Cosmos and the Creator: Introduction to the Theology of Creation.* London: SPCK, 1998.

Gunton, Colin E. *The Doctrine of Creation.* London: Continuum, 2004.

———. *The Triune Creator: A Historical and Systematic Study.* Grand Rapids: Eerdmans, 1998.

Jarvis, Peter. *Ecological Principles and Environmental Issues.* Upper Saddle River, NJ: Prentice Hall, 2000.

Moltmann, Jürgen. *God in Creation: An Ecological Doctrine of Creation.* London: SCM, 1985.

Schmemann, Alexander. *The World as Sacrament,* new edition. London: Darton, Longman & Todd, 1974.

4 The Incarnation

An Affirmation of True Humanity

The fact that God became flesh — i.e., a concrete human being or one of us — in Christ is the turning point of the history of salvation, and thus the center of Christian faith. At the same time, it includes a strong affirmation of the preciousness of creation as well as of all true and real humanity. And it reminds us that there is no aspect of our human existence and no part of the earth — not even the darkest prison or the most severe misery — unless Christ has been there before us and remains with us. This is the sure foundation of our hope. In all these respects, the incarnation is essential to a materialist spirituality.

God's becoming flesh in Jesus Christ is the great marvel or wonder of the Christian faith. Yet, it did not happen in a particularly striking or glorious manner. There is no burning bush here, as with Moses. No tongues of fire, no powerful signs, not even a silent breeze or "a still small voice" as in the case of Elijah (1 Kings 19:12). The most extraordinary feature of the nativity story is actually that it occurs in such an ordinary and common way. Jesus was born as a poor child in a poor family, under conditions similar to the vast majority of children at that time — and also today. His father, Joseph the carpenter, and his mother, Mary the young teenage girl, were struggling with the same insecurity in facing the future as most parents. And even if angels descended on the fields of Bethlehem, adding heavenly song to the event, and three kings came from far, offering the newborn child precious gifts, the whole thing took place in a miserable little shed where God's Son was laid in a shabby crib.

These circumstances aim at showing that Jesus came into the world as one of us, within the framework of an all-embracing and nearly inconceivable act of solidarity. They also point to a crucial element in his work as a whole: It is precisely through his humanity that Christ can save us human beings. He became our brother in everything, but without being defeated by sin. This is why he was able to "(bear) our sins in his body on the tree, that we might die to sin and live to righteousness. By his wounds (we) have been healed" (1 Peter 2:24).

The New Testament contains several beautiful and vigorous expressions of the wonder of the incarnation and its central implications:

> The true light that enlightens every man was coming into the world. He was in the world, and the world was made through him, yet the world knew him not. He came to his own home, but his own people received him not. But to all who received him, who believed in his name, he gave power to become children of God; who were born, not of blood nor of the will of the flesh nor of the will of man, but of God. And the Word became flesh and dwelt among us, full of grace and truth; we have beheld his glory, glory as of the only Son from the Father. (John 1:9-14)

> Have this mind among yourselves, which is yours in Christ Jesus, who, though he was in the form of God, did not count equality with God a thing to be grasped, but emptied himself, taking the form of a servant, being born in the likeness of men. And being found in human form he humbled himself and became obedient unto death, even death on a cross. Therefore God has highly exalted him and bestowed on him the name which is above every name, that at the name of Jesus every knee should bow, in heaven and on earth and under the earth, and every tongue confess that Jesus Christ is Lord, to the glory of God the Father. (Phil. 2:5-11)

> For you know the grace of our Lord Jesus Christ, that though he was rich, yet for your sake he became poor, so that by his poverty you might become rich. (2 Cor. 8:9)

The church expresses central parts of its faith in the incarnated Christ through the doctrine of his two natures. This doctrine affirms that Christ is very God from eternity and in that sense equal with the Father. But he is also wholly and truly human, being our brother in everything. As the experience from the Old Church affirms, these natures should neither be torn apart nor muddled together. Also in his post-resurrection existence, Christ is fully human. Yet, while his humanity is embraced by divinity and this divinity is carried by the same humanity, his divinity is never transformed or changed into humanity. The best and most authentic exposition of the doctrine of the two natures in Christ can be found in the early sixth-century Athanasian Creed, where the person of Christ is seen in the perspective of the Trinity. Here it is further stated:

> For the right Faith is, that we believe and confess: that our Lord
>   Jesus Christ, the Son of God, is God and Man;
> God, of the substance of the Father; begotten before the worlds:
>   and Man, of the Substance of his Mother,
>   born in the world.
> Perfect God: and perfect Man, of a reasonable soul
>   and human flesh subsisting.
> Equal to the Father, as touching his Godhead: and inferior
>   to the Father as touching his Manhood.
> Who although he be God and Man; yet he is not two,
>   but one Christ.
> One; not by conversion of the Godhead into flesh:
>   but by taking of the Manhood into God.
> One altogether; not by confusion of Substance: but by unity
>   of Person.
> For as the reasonable soul and flesh is one man:
>   so God and Man is one Christ. . . .
>   (here quoted from the *Book of Common Prayer*)

The insistence that Jesus was born of a virgin — or the virgin birth — plays a key role in this connection. The fact that the Son of God was born of Mary emphasizes his true humanity; while the corresponding fact that this took place through the Holy Spirit without the participation of a man reflects his equally true divinity. Meticulous speculations on what the virgin birth may imply in biological terms should probably be avoided. (I still remember a disturbing incident from my youth

when I heard someone fervently defending this article of faith by referring to similar occurrences among turkeys!) Yet, this part of the
church's tradition corresponds to and supports the indispensable doctrine of the two natures in Christ. In this capacity, the present teaching
becomes highly significant, too. I have already suggested that the Holy
Virgin — the teenage girl who became the Mother of God — in many
respects is crucial to a materialist spirituality. In addition to the female
perspective, Mary actualizes the soundly human dimension of faith.
She is not an object of prayer or devotion in herself, but she is honored
as the *theotokos*. And being the one who gave birth to Jesus, she also becomes the mother of the church and all the faithful. We, therefore, ask
for her intercession and care. That will hardly be harmful to anyone.

Christ's humanity has often been lying as a kind of cover or veil
over his witness. This was the case with some of those who were first
confronted with his message — knowing that the person who employed
such big words actually was the son of the carpenter down the street. It
also applies to many of us who hear the gospel today — often longing
for something more grandiose, palpable, and convincing. We look for
proofs that may remove the torturous ambiguity of our faith, something
that can counteract the doubt that nags us.

At the same time, the incarnation reflects the almost overpower-
ing logic of salvation, as expressed by Anselm of Canterbury in the elev-
enth century: Humans needed to atone for their break against the creator and his good will for creation. However, only one who was God
could deliver such atonement. Thus, God had to become a human being. There was simply no other way if humankind was to be saved and
creation redeemed. And who knows — the plain narrative of Christ's
act of solidarity may in the end speak just as strongly as more conspicuous forms of religiosity.

Materialist spirituality must always be understood as an incarnational
spirituality — thus, firmly anchored in the central foundation of our
faith. I shall now turn to the implications of the incarnation in view of
our spiritual life. Here I will have to restrict myself to pointing briefly
at five basic concerns:

First, I have already noted that God's becoming a human being in
Christ implies an affirmation of all true humanity. The incarnation not
only confirms the worth of human nature; it also provides the founda-

tion for a restoration of endangered or lost humanity. Such an affirmation has a significant bearing in regard to our spirituality. It shows that our lives must be marked by openness towards and respect for all things that mediate such humanity — and by a readiness to stand up in defense of corresponding ideals, especially in a time when they are jeopardized. Christian faith does not mean that human nature is denied or annulled, but that it is verified and perfected. And it would be rather awkward if we should withdraw from humanity and its consequences, while Christ — the cornerstone of our faith — came and comes to us as our brother.

A corresponding approach is reflected in the hymn of the great Danish theologian and hymn-writer N. F. S. Grundtvig, "Menneske først og Christen saa" ("Human first and Christian next"). As far as I know, this stunning hymn from the early nineteenth century has not been translated into English. But its key concern is the close interaction between humanity and Christianity. Yet another manifestation of the humanistic dimension of Christian faith can be found in Philippians 4:8: "Whatever is true, whatever is honorable, whatever is just, whatever is pure, whatever is lovely, whatever is gracious, if there is any excellence, if there is anything worthy of praise, think about these things." Here we see that our life as Christians is not anchored solely in religious deeds in a narrow sense, but also in general human virtues. Along these lines, we are once more reminded of a striking newspaper headline: Do as God, become human!

Now, my emphasis on what can be labeled as Christian humanism does not suggest that all human acts should or can be recognized as expressions of true humanity. Regrettably, we often constitute the most serious threat in this area ourselves — partly by ignoring the humanity of others and partly by a practice that imperils our own humanity. Christ's affirmation of human dignity therefore contains a critical perspective — counteracting behavior and attitudes that put such dignity at jeopardy. His message to the woman who had been caught in adultery includes a strong and merciful affirmation, but also a challenge: ". . . go, and do not sin again" (John 8:11). Thus seen, humanity is not a static entity; it requires careful cultivation. A central aim here is plain human decency, in keeping with the Golden Rule: "So whatever you wish that men would do to you, do so to them" (Matt. 7:12).

Subsequently, it must be underscored that the relationship between humanism and Christianity is supposed to work both ways too. Just as impulses from humanism add significantly to the Christian faith, several adaptations of this faith form essential contributions to the larger humanistic tradition. There is a deep fellowship in morals and values in these two currents. A humanism that denounces Christianity is just as truncated as anti-humanistic versions of faith. Similarly, a militantly secularized humanism can under certain circumstances be just as potentially dangerous as its militant Christian counterparts. A proper balance is needed.

Second, as an incarnational form of piety, materialist spirituality is heavily conditioned by the flesh or by the concrete human existence in its fullness and richness. These entities form the main framework of our spiritual life. Admittedly, an ambiguity in regard to the flesh can be noticed in the New Testament — also seeing it as the opposite of our life in the Spirit. However, this depends on the fall and the influence of sin. It does not in any sense invalidate the solid affirmation of the human "flesh" essential to the incarnation, especially since the fruits of the Spirit are perceived as human virtues. Moreover, falsely spiritualized or Gnostically inclined options are consistently rejected — stressing that we are being saved as bodies. In the wake of this, bigotry, insularity, and narrow prejudices as well as deeply anti-cultural and anti-modernist attitudes must also be avoided. Generally, nothing that is truly human should be foreign to us, only those factors that threaten true humanity. Or — as Paul puts it: "'All things are lawful for me,' but not all things are helpful. 'All things are lawful for me,' but I will not be enslaved by anything" (1 Cor. 6:12). Seen in this perspective, an incarnationally anchored spirituality should be accompanied by cultural commitment, human generosity, and openness to the world.

This directs us once more towards the limitless solidarity and compassion that distinguishes the incarnation of Christ. He descended from heaven and entered the ultimate confines of human existence — even the realm of death — to secure that we should "become partakers of the divine nature" (2 Peter 1:4). He became poor in order that we should become rich (cf. the already quoted 2 Cor. 8:9). And — in the words of an Old Testament prophecy: ". . . he bore the sin of many" (Isa. 53:12). This is what Martin Luther refers to as the "holy exchange": Christ takes our sins upon him and in return makes us partakers in the justification he won at the cross. But this event can also be described as an act of boundless solidarity. Such solidarity is also obligatory to a materialist spirituality. Hence, there can be no true spirituality without love — the bond that "binds everything together in perfect harmony" (Col. 3:14).

Third, the incarnation is not only about the saving of souls. Quite on the contrary, it must be interpreted as a highly significant step towards the redemption of creation and God's world. Christ is "the light of the world" (John 8:12); he is "the bread . . . which . . . gives life to the world" (John 6:33). It is further his task to "unite all things in him, things in heaven and things on earth" (Eph. 1:10). This reflects the immense cosmic scope of Christ's work. And it affirms what I have said in the previous chapter about the interrelatedness of creation and redemption in God's plan for salvation. Thus, incarnational spirituality always comes across as a creation-based spirituality.

Fourth, materialist spirituality is aware that the fact of Christ's becoming a human being can be a stumbling block, something that entices us to doubt that he is able to deliver. His message has been met by such sentiments from the beginning. Today, a tempting alternative is offered by theologies that sell personal prosperity and well-being. Such alternatives, however, are in acute danger of developing into a shallow form of Christian triumphalism in which both the humanity of Christ and his suffering at the cross are toned down. Authentic Christianity never takes us around agony — as the so-called *Bøyg* or "bend" in Henrik Ibsen's *Peer Gynt* commends, but holds the promise of being able to lead us through pain. This compares to the so-called "law of the kernel of wheat": Something must fall to the ground and die if new life is to come forth (cf. John 12:24). It also corresponds with the essential biblical principle that "[God's] power is made perfect in weakness" (2 Cor. 12:9). Accordingly, attitudes that in effect imply that the true humanity of Christ and his suffering are neglected or even denied have heretical implications.

God does not exercise his rule by raw force, but primarily through love and compassion. And love can always be rejected. Subsequently, materialist spirituality aims at leading us into the way of humility. This is a part of our imitation of Christ. In the view of St. Bernard, meekness is the starting point of self-insight. And the Benedictine Anselm Grün describes humbleness as a descent into our own reality. At the same time, the principle that God's power is perfected in weakness also reflects that God is fully capable of transforming the weakest and most timid human beings into eager and committed witnesses to the gospel. The history of the church is brimming with examples of this — starting with Peter, the denier who became the rock. Humility should therefore not be confused with lingering feebleness or unconditional surrender. It can be far more potent than assumed at first glance. This is due to the fact that it entails participation in the power of the cross, which — despite its lack of worldly power — has proved to be invincible. We, therefore, exclaim: *Ave crux, spes unica;* praised be the cross, our only hope.

Fifth, an incarnationally anchored materialist spirituality presupposes that the Christ who came into the world as a human being continues to be incarnated in the reality of the church which is his body on earth (cf. Johann Adam Möhler et al.). This takes place through the vibrant mediation of the Holy Spirit. It occurs in the concrete space of the church. And it has the sacraments as its main signs or instruments. Accordingly, the wonder of the incarnation also provides the foundation of our ecclesiology and sacramental theology. This does not suggest that Christ and his church can be flatly identified; it is more a question of presence — a very real and palpable presence. Within the sphere of the church, the basically invisible nature of our hope is transcended — primarily through its sacramental celebration, but also through its sign language as a whole. These vital concerns will be further explored in the ensuing chapters.

In concluding my regrettably brief account of the Christological anchoring of a materialist spirituality, I will once more turn to literature. In the moving novel *Silence* by the Japanese Catholic author Shusaku Endo, we find an expression of the deep solidarity and the liberating powers that are reflected in and through the incarnation. The novel focuses on the persecutions that the faithful and the foreign missionaries were exposed to in seventeenth-century Japan. Under threats of death penalty, they were forced to trample on pictures of Christ. In the following citation, Endo recounts a meeting between the Portuguese priest Father Rodrigues and Kichijiro, one of those who had abandoned his faith:

> When the man looked toward the priest, their eyes met. It was Kichijiro. For a moment a spasm of fear crossed that face and Kichijiro retreated backwards a few steps.

"Father!" His voice was like the whining of a dog. "Father! Listen to me!"

The priest withdrew his face from the window and tried to block his ears to the sound of that voice. How could he ever forget the dried fish, the burning thirst in his throat. Even if he tried to forgive the fellow, he could not drive from his memory the hatred and anger that lurked there.

[. . .]

The priest closed his eyes and began to recite the *Credo*. He felt a sense of joy being able to abandon this whimpering fellow in the rain. Even though Christ prayed, Judas had hanged himself in the field of blood — and had Christ prayed for Judas? There was nothing about that in the Scriptures; and even if there was, he could not put himself into such a frame of mind as to be able to do likewise. In any case, to what extent could the fellow be trusted? He was looking for pardon; but this perhaps was no more than a passing moment of excitement.

[. . .]

"Father, father!" Seeing that the priest had come to the prison, Kichijiro was again pleading in the darkness. "Let me confess my sins and repent!"

The priest had no right to refuse the sacrament of penance to anyone. If a person asked for the sacrament, it was not for him to concede or refuse according to his own feelings. He raised his hand in blessing, uttered dutifully the prescribed prayer and put his ear close to the other. As the foul breath was wafted into his face, there in the darkness the vision of the yellow teeth and the crafty look floated before his eyes.

"Listen to me, Father," Kichijiro whimpered in a voice that the other Christians could hear. "I am an apostate; but if I had died ten years ago I might have gone to paradise as a good Christian, not despised as an apostate. Merely because I live in a time of persecution. . . . I am sorry."

"But do you still believe?" asked the priest, doing his best to put up with the foul stench of the other's breath. "I will give you absolution, but I cannot trust you. I cannot understand why you have come here."

Heaving a deep sigh and searching for words of explanation,

Kichijiro shifted and shuffled. The stench of his filth and sweat was wafted toward the priest. Could it be possible that Christ loved and searched after this dirtiest of men? In evil there remained that strength and beauty of evil; but this Kichijiro was not even worthy to be called evil. He was thin and dirty like the tattered rags he wore. Suppressing his disgust, the priest recited the final words of absolution, and then, following the established custom, he whispered, "Go in peace." With all possible speed getting away from the stench of that mouth and that body, he returned to where the Christians were.

No, no. Our Lord had searched out the ragged and the dirty. Thus he reflected as he lay in bed. Among the people who appeared in the pages of the Scripture, those whom Christ had searched after in love were the woman of Capernaum with the issue of blood, the woman taken in adultery whom men had wanted to stone — people with no attraction, no beauty. Anyone could be attracted by the beautiful and charming. But could such attraction be called love? True love was to accept humanity when wasted like rags and tatters. Theoretically the priest knew all this; but still he could not forgive Kichijiro. Once again near his face came the face of Christ, wet with tears. When the gentle eyes looked straight into his, the priest was filled with shame. (*Silence*, pp. 185-89)

Similar concerns are communicated in the writings of other twentieth-century authors who stand in the Catholic tradition, such as Graham Greene, Georges Bernanos, Morris West, Miguel de Unamuno, and their Norwegian colleague Åge Rønning. In several of their novels, there is a frightening awareness of the persistence of evil. At the same time, they demonstrate that the incarnated Christ transgresses the borders of evil. Moreover, he is fully able to transform the most depraved or even repulsive human beings and restore their dignity. And while just about anybody can love the attractive and successful, it takes a God to love those who are the opposite — foul, horrendous, and revolting. Greene's *The Power and the Glory*, Bernanos' *The Diary of a Country Priest*, and Unamuno's *Saint Manuel Bueno, Martyr* are all examples of this. Here we witness how weak and vulnerable persons grow to be agents of what is good and right.

This is not at all about salvation by works. It rather reflects the immense potential of Christ and his grace in our lives. And it adjusts the proclivity towards a one-sidedly negative anthropology that marks some theologies. These concerns correspond to what was said in the previous chapter about the capacity of grace to perfect human nature and the dialectic between what Christ does *for* us and *in* us. Surely, the *sola gratia* principle must not be understood as excluding or ignoring the effects of a liberating divine presence in our lives.

As Endo and his author colleagues show us, however, the most important implication of a spirituality anchored in the unshakeable reality of the incarnation is the assurance that Christ never leaves us. He is always with us — in all aspects of our human life and even in the deepest valleys of despair. This basic assurance is absolutely essential to all viable spiritualities.

Literature

Brown, Raymond. *An Introduction to New Testament Christology.* Mahwah, NJ: Paulist Press, 2005.

Dunn, James G. *Christology in the Making: An Inquiry into the Origins of the Doctrine of the Incarnation,* 3rd revised version. London: SCM, 2003.

Endo, Shusaku. *Silence.* Translated by William Johnston. Tokyo, New York, London: Kodansha International, 1982.

Grün, Anselm. *Jesus: The Image of Humanity.* London: Continuum, 2003.

Irenaeus of Lyon. *The Scandal of the Incarnation.* Selected and introduced by Hans Urs von Balthasar. San Francisco: Ignatius Press, 1990.

Kasper, Walter. *Jesus the Christ.* Mahwah, NJ: Paulist Press, 2005.

McCarthy, Timothy. *Christianity and Humanism: From Their Biblical Foundations into the Third Millennium.* Chicago: Loyola Press, 1996.

O'Collins, Gerald. *Christology: A Biblical, Historical and Systematic Study of Jesus Christ.* Oxford: Oxford University Press, 1995.

O'Collins, Gerald, ed. *Incarnation.* London: Continuum, 2002.

Vanier, Jean. *Becoming Human.* Mahwah, NJ: Paulist Press, 1999.

Whitehouse, J. C. *Vertical Man: The Human Being in the Catholic Novels of Graham Greene, Sigrid Undset, and Georges Bernanos.* New York: Garland Publishing, 1990.

5 The Holy Spirit

The Grounded Wire of Christian Life

The Holy Spirit is the breath of our life in Christ and adds vibrancy to this life. He is further the sign and bond that the age of salvation has dawned. He grants us freedom from the law in our pursuit of redemption — sustaining faith, hope, and love within and among us. He is the foundation of our status as God's children. And he equips us to live to the honor of God and the benefit of all our neighbors. These points demonstrate that the new life in faith we are called to is a life in the Spirit. Accordingly, the witness to the Holy Spirit in Scripture and tradition is an essential and indispensable building block in all forms of piety: There can be no true spirituality without the presence of the Spirit.

Yet, hardly any part of church doctrine has been exposed to such a shifting or even sad destiny as pneumatology. Within classic Western theologies like the Catholic and the Reformation traditions, it must be admitted that the Holy Spirit has been somewhat marginalized. This becomes evident in dogmatic expositions as well as the practice of these churches. At the same time, currents that are strongly concerned with pneumatology often appear to be in danger of confusing the works of the Spirit with a particular pattern of human experiences or ecstatic emotions. This is not least the case within the many neo-charismatic groups that have been popping up during the last decades. Here one gets the impression that the longing to be filled by the Spirit has tipped over into a restless pursuit of forever new and stronger spiritualized sensations.

54

The need for changes in and a renewal of pneumatology thus seems evident. At this point, fruitful impulses can be found in the Eastern Orthodox churches, which have been far more concerned with this part of theology. Traditional Pentecostalism will often have something to offer in this field, too. The point of departure for such renewal must be that the Holy Spirit forms the basis or framework of our actual and daily Christian existence. This existence is not about a narrow religious sphere or tremulous experiences. Life in the Spirit is our life in the world as Christians. Hence, pneumatology should not be treated as a religious cabinet of oddities. Here the point is the blatant opposite — namely that the Spirit is the solid foundation or the grounded wire of our life in Christ.

This compares to central features in the biblical account of the Holy Spirit. In this connection, Paul's account of the fruits of the Spirit is crucial:

> But I say, walk by the Spirit, and do not gratify the desires of the flesh. For the desires of the flesh are against the Spirit, and the desires of the Spirit are against the flesh; for these are opposed to each other, to prevent you from doing what you would. But if you are led by the Spirit you are not under the law. Now, the works of the flesh are plain: fornication, impurity, licentiousness, idolatry, sorcery, enmity, strife, jealousy, anger, selfishness, dissension, party spirit, envy, drunkenness, carousing, and the like. I warn you, as I warned you before, that those who do such things shall not inherit the kingdom of God. But the fruit of the Spirit is love, joy, peace, patience, kindness, goodness, faithfulness, gentleness, self-control; against such there is no law. And those who belong to Christ Jesus have crucified the flesh with its passions and desires.
>
> If we live by the Spirit, let us also walk by the Spirit. Let us have no self-conceit, no provoking of one another, no envy of one another. (Gal. 5:16-26)

This exposition shows that the fight against sin is conducted by living a life in the Spirit. And this life plays a key role in our efforts to restore true humanity, in correspondence with the will of the creator. We have already noted that the fruits of the Spirit are attached to plain human virtues like love, peace, patience, kindness, and self-control. Here there are no traces of ecstatic peculiarities. Such virtues can be characterized as "ecumenical," in the sense that they are particularly relevant in view of the building of human — and ecclesial — community. The things that threaten our life in the Spirit, however, impede fellowship: enmity, strife, jealousy, anger, selfishness, etc. On this background, it can be deduced that the Holy Spirit contributes significantly to a life in unity and solidarity. The work of the Spirit should, therefore, be seen as fundamental to the church's calling to stand forth as the first-fruit of a re-united humankind. This is reflected in the reference to the unifying spiritual language that points towards the restoration of the fellowship that was lost at the tower of Babel (cf. Acts 2:1-13). Here the Holy Spirit also meets us as the Spirit of communication, being vital to the church's mission in the world.

Trying to explore this further, three important aspects of the Holy Spirit's work must be emphasized: First, the Spirit is a concrete person within the framework of the Trinity. As a divine being, he is worshiped together with the Father and the Son. Admittedly, the person-concept has special connotations here — the Spirit is not a person in the same way as we are. Yet, the use of this concept signifies that the Holy Spirit cannot be downgraded to the level of pure emotions, spiritualized sentiments, or ecstatic experiences. Quite on the contrary, the Spirit is a divine person with clearly defined tasks within the drama of salvation.

In the wake of this, something must be said about the Trinitarian foundation of theology in general — partly based on observations from this and the two previous chapters. Christian faith is essentially Trinitarian; it is always expressed as faith in the Father, the Son, and the Spirit. This is the context of the role of the Holy Spirit as a divine person. More concretely, the church's tradition here talks about one divine being or substance and three distinct persons. These persons should be neither torn apart nor mixed together. God is thus triune; he is both one and three — and he is this simultaneously and invariably. In this way, the Trinitarian dogma reflects the basic unity as well as the richness and comprehensiveness of our image of God. The dogma is also relevant to our spiritual life: We believe in the Father who is the creator of all; we believe in the Son who is our redeemer; and we believe in the Spirit who is the giver of life. If one of the divine persons is marginalized, our confession becomes incomplete and deficient. A faith that is marked by an intense focus on Christ may appear as deceptively pious. Still, a materialist spirituality presupposes that our faith in Christ is kept firmly together with the dimension of creation. This also applies to the Holy Spirit. Accordingly, authentic spirituality is marked by a consistent Trinitarian balance, in which all three divine persons and their work are accounted for. Heresies frequently depend on this balance being lost.

Second, both the scriptures and church tradition describe the Holy Spirit as the spokesman or the counselor of Christ — i.e., the divine person who makes Christ concretely present as savior, also after his ascent to heaven:

> "I have yet many things to say to you, but you cannot bear them now. When the Spirit of truth comes, he will guide you into all the truth; for he will not speak on his own authority, but whatever he hears he will speak, and he will declare to you the things that are to come. He will glorify me, for he will take what is mine and declare it to you. All that the Father has is mine; therefore I said that he will take what is mine and declare it to you." (John 16:12-15)

As the spokesman of Christ and as "the Spirit of truth," the Holy Spirit is basically where Christ is. This implies that our life in Christ is a life in the Spirit, and that our life in the Spirit is a life in Christ. At the core of this is the assurance that salvation in Christ becomes ours through the Holy Spirit. This insoluble bond between Christ and his Spirit is the main criterion in view of our distinction between what is of the Spirit and what is not of the Spirit:

> Beloved, do not believe every spirit, but test the spirits to see whether they are of God; for many false prophets have gone out into the world. By this you know the Spirit of God: every spirit which confesses that Jesus Christ has come in the flesh is of God, and every spirit which does not confess Jesus is not of God. This is the spirit of antichrist, of which you heard that it was coming, and now it is in the world already. (1 John 4:1-3)

Ecumenically and historically speaking, there are many arguments in favor of skipping the *filioque* of the Nicene Creed — the formulation that maintains that the Spirit proceeds from the Father *and the Son*. One such argument is to avoid narrow christomonism. Yet, the Western tradition has a valid point in stressing the relationship between Christ and the Spirit — being both *Spiritus creator*, the Spirit of creation, and *Spiritus Christi*. This should not be forgotten, particularly not as pneumatology has developed lately. Generally, the Holy Spirit is always clear and lucid. Our spiritual sentiments, however, can be fairly ambiguous and rugged. This is the reason why we have to learn to test the spirits. And such testing must take place within the context of a solid confession of Christ.

Third, the Holy Spirit does not work in thin air or within a spiritual vacuum. The Spirit's work rather takes place through concrete and empirically perceptible means and within an equally concrete space. Here the word of God — i.e., the outward word that we hear read and preached, especially in the service of the church — and the visible sacraments play a key role. This is *inter alia* confirmed by the fact that our baptism in the Spirit or the so-called spiritual baptism always takes place through water. Furthermore, all the means of grace are administered within the realm of the church — at the same time constituting and so to speak creating the church. This reflects that the Holy Spirit does not only deal with us as individual faithful. The Spirit is also — or even mainly — the Spirit of the whole community, the Spirit who bestows life on the body of the church and makes it the place of salvation. In this field, Catholic and classical Reformation theology stand together in the conviction that the Holy Spirit grants our participation in salvation in Christ through outwardly recognizable means and in a concrete space. This is a vital implication of article V of the Augsburg Confession — in my view the chief article of this important confessional writing:

> That we may obtain this faith, the Ministry of Teaching the Gospel and administering the Sacraments was instituted. For through the Word and the Sacraments, as through instruments, the Holy Ghost is given, who works faith; where and when it pleases God, in them that hear the Gospel, to wit, that God, not for our merits, but for Christ's sake, justifies those who believe that they are received into grace for Christ's sake.
>
> They condemn the Anabaptists and others who think that the Holy Ghost comes to men without the external Word, through their own preparations and works.

Seen in light of this concern as well as the two previous ones, it can be argued that pneumatology also affirms and expresses the concrete corporeality of Christian faith. In this respect, it clearly corresponds with the theology of creation and Christology. And it points towards a materialist spirituality.

In examining the role of the Holy Spirit in Christian life further, the so-called charismata or gifts of grace are of fundamental importance. These gifts primarily appear as a Pauline concern. Even if the Johannine writings have much to say about the Holy Spirit, they contain hardly any references to the special spiritual charismata — let alone their more ecstatic adaptations. Still, these gifts were central in the early church. And representing a way to spiritual enrichment and renewal, we cannot afford to ignore them. It is thus deplorable that the charismatic dimension traditionally has played a rather modest role within most of the mainline churches. At the same time, the gifts of grace should not be identified with extraordinary, ecstatic, and emotionally directed phenomena like prophecy, speaking in tongues, and healing. Paul also describes the exercise of leadership and "the utterance of wisdom . . . and knowledge" as charismata (cf. 1 Cor. 12:7-8). He further states that "in the church I would rather speak five words with my mind, in order to instruct others, than ten thousand words in a tongue" (1 Cor. 14:19). In comparison with the more conspicuous gifts, practical and down-to-earth love is actually the most important one:

> If I speak in the tongues of men and angels, but have no love, I am a noisy gong or a clanging cymbal. And if I have prophetic power, and understand all mysteries, and all knowledge, and if I have all faith, so as to remove mountains, but have not love, I am nothing. [. . .]
>
> Love is patient and kind; love is not jealous or boastful; it is not arrogant or rude. Love does not insist on its own way; it is not irritable or resentful; it does not rejoice at wrong, but rejoices in the right. Love bears all things, believes all things, hopes all things, endures all things.
>
> Love never ends; as for prophecies, they will pass away; as for tongues, they will cease; as for knowledge, it will pass away. For our knowledge is imperfect and our prophecy is imperfect; but when the perfect comes, the imperfect will pass away. [. . .] So faith,

hope, love abide, these three; but the greatest of these is love.
(1 Cor. 13:1-13)

Paul was probably some sort of charismatic himself. He had been endowed with a number of spiritual gifts, including ecstatic ones. Yet, he never succumbed to either the triumphalism of a theology of glory or any urge to deny the severe realities of life. In the middle of his spiritual strength, this giant of faith presents himself as a sick and often quite helpless charismatic:

> . . . to keep me from being too elated by the abundance of revelations, a thorn was given me in the flesh, a messenger of Satan, to harass me, to keep me from being too elated. Three times I besought the Lord about this, that it should leave me; but he said to me, "My grace is sufficient for you, for my power is made perfect in weakness." I will all the more gladly boast of my weakness, that the power of Christ may rest upon me. For the sake of Christ, then, I am content with weakness, insults, hardships, persecutions, and calamities; for when I am weak, then I am strong. (2 Cor. 12:7-10)

In Paul's view, the most crucial feature of a gift of grace is not its extraordinary character, but rather that it contributes to building up the church: ". . . since you are eager for manifestations of the Spirit, strive to excel in building up the church" (1 Cor. 14:12). Moreover: "When you come together, each one has a hymn, a lesson, a revelation, a tongue, or an interpretation. Let all things be done for edification" (1 Cor. 14:26). Here the apostle addresses an attitude that implies that the gifts of grace were used to the end of private spiritual consumption. This attitude often led to the manufacturing of a religious hierarchy where some looked upon themselves as more "spiritual" than others. Such postures still exist. Paul, however, claims that the Holy Spirit opposes all proclivities towards spiritual pretentiousness — insisting that the charismatic gifts shall and must promote common growth and true unity in the church's life.

At this point, the concept of the body is fundamental. The church is Christ's body; and within this body all the parts work together for the common good. Paul's detailed account of the present concept in 1 Corinthians 12 includes several crucial observations: First, the apostle sees the church as Christ's body in a very concrete sense. Even the somewhat shaky and far from perfect congregation of Corinth is depicted in this way: "Now you *are* the body of Christ and individually members of it" (v. 27). This not only applies to brief glorious moments, but is a fact as long as Christ remains among them. Second, the Spirit emerges as the "glue" of the church in binding its different members and their charismata together in a mutually committed fellowship: ". . . there are varieties of gifts, but the same Spirit" (v. 4); and "all these are inspired by one and the same Spirit, who apportions to each one individually as he wills" (v. 11). Third, this happens not least through the sacraments as visible instruments or signs: "For by one Spirit we were all baptized into one body . . . and all were made to drink of one Spirit" (v. 13). While the reference to baptism here is evident, the drinking of one Spirit presumably alludes to the Eucharist.

The one body of the church is distinguished by the fact that all false and unnecessary human borderlines are canceled and transgressed: As faithful we share in one Spirit and one spiritual life — "Jews or Greeks, slaves or free" alike (v. 13). Subsequently, all fake religious hierarchies are excluded, together with the spiritual flamboyance that such hierarchies lead to: ". . . the parts of the body which seem to be weaker are indispensable" (v. 22). Further, ". . . God has so composed the body, giving the greater honor to the inferior part, that there may be no discord in the body, but that the members may have the same care for one another" (vv. 24f.). All these points are expressions of the infinite care and solidarity that shall mark the life of the church: "If one member suffers, all suffer together; if one member is honored, all rejoice together" (v. 26).

A more stunningly beautiful and appropriate account of the church than the one that is given in 1 Corinthians 12 can hardly be envisioned. Yet, its beauty never moves towards fogginess and uncommitted chatter. Here we are talking about a life that is marked by order, stability, and sound common sense — also stressing our elementary and bodily needs. Paul does not settle with an ideal picture of the church. The life in the body of Christ includes a persistent battle against selfishness as well as spiritual arrogance; and it presupposes that we are ready to fulfill the law of Christ by carrying each other's burdens (cf. Gal. 6:2). Behind all of this stands the Holy Spirit, who binds our multiple gifts and differences together within a communal framework of solidarity and compassion. As we shall see in a later chapter, this does not mean that diversity is excluded. But it signifies that the Spirit makes us grow together towards Christ, and thus towards ever more unity and fellowship.

What, then, with the extraordinary spiritual gifts? I do not want to be overly polemical at this point. There can be little doubt that the mainline churches have much to learn from segments of the charismatic movement. Yet, quite a few of the neo-charismatic groups expose biases and problematic developments that threaten to disguise or invalidate their potential. On the one hand, charismatics are correct in claiming that the life in the Spirit includes special and partly ecstatic spiritual experiences. On the other hand, we have seen that this life is not identical with or limited to such phenomena. What is at stake here is actually something far greater and richer than this, being firmly embedded in the center of our life and our everyday existence. The neo-charismatic movement frequently appears to aim at removing or estranging people from reality, through noise and upheaval. As opposed to this, a materialist spirituality insists that our Christian life first and foremost is grounded in the world of God the creator. Along such lines, the inclination to confuse our faith in the Holy Spirit — the Spirit of life — with a rather narrow spectrum of spiritualized sentiments and shallow effects is adjusted.

Further, neo-charismatics are right in arguing that the Holy Spirit deals with us as persons. Still, we have already noted that the Spirit cannot be flatly identified with particular emotional patterns or ecstatic happenings. At worst, this may lead to God the Holy Spirit being anthropologized or falsely muddled together with an all-too-human spirit. That was certainly not the point, regardless of how personally earthshaking our spiritual experiences may seem. In the wake of this, it should be underscored that the Holy Spirit is also the Spirit of fellowship and the Spirit of the church. And the Spirit's gifts never stop with individuals; they are always directed towards building community.

Within the more extreme neo-charismatic groups, there is a tendency to use or sell powerful spiritual sensations as ingredients for private religious consumption. Here a whole spiral of experiences is applied, being turned higher and higher towards a culmination with rather bizarre results. The goal of this is to compete with media in offering people even stronger vibes than they get in front of the TV with its endless number of channels. Within such frameworks, there is little room for the biblical principle that "power is made perfect in weakness" (2 Cor. 12:9) — actualizing the temptation of triumphalism and glory theology. I regret to have to say this, but in my opinion the pursuit of thrilling experiences confirms that the expression, "empty barrels make most noise," applies also in the religious sphere, in a most literal sense.

A possible reason for my harsh criticism may be that a documentary about the so-called Jesus-camp — or the "Kids on Fire Summer Camp" of Pastor Becky Fischer and her frantic associates — was recently featured on Norwegian television. It was shocking to watch this film, which showed how kids were turned into "children soldiers" for President Bush and Jesus — in that order, it seemed. A detestation of the values of others was eagerly promoted, through loud noise and shallow political-religious agitation, with the now-retired and disgraced evangelical leader Ted Haggard appearing as an enthusiastic supporter of the exercises. I am aware that this may be a more extreme charismatic branch. Yet, such extremes are highly appealing to a vast and steadily growing number of people — not only in the U.S. but around the world. And they are effectively fueled by militant populism. Not least in this perspective, the challenge as well as the promise of a materialist spirituality becomes absolutely imperative.

According to the Nicene Creed, the Holy Spirit is the Lord and giver of life — *Dominum et vivificantem,* i.e., the divine person who invigorates both God's people and the whole of creation. The Spirit is, therefore, associated with the dynamic aspects of Christian life, also contributing to openness and creativity. This is a vital point. The Holy Spirit works sustainable renewal and frees us from narrow-mindedness and insularity. Yet, this concern needs further precision. For dynamism is not the same as chaos. As Paul affirms in 1 Corinthians 12, we are called to behave in a sane, sensible, and basically decent way — being, you might say, "spiritual fruits" and not "religious nuts." And as already pointed out, pneumatology should not be treated as a theological cabinet of peculiarities.

It is occasionally argued that the Spirit's role as the dynamic giver of life implies a tension over against the ecclesial institution. Now, the Holy Spirit cannot be fully identified with the church and its structures. Still, we have seen that the Spirit particularly is at work within the church, which is the location of salvation — constituting, invigorating, and equipping it for its mission. There is thus an ecclesiological and institutional dimension to pneumatology. This does not mean that the Holy Spirit is solely present in the church. He is also the Spirit of creation and works in creation. And he constantly prompts the church to reach out across its borders. But the saving acts of the Spirit have the church as its central space. Here he works through outwardly and empirically perceptible means — i.e., through the word we hear, through the water that runs over our head in baptism, and through what we eat and drink in the Eucharist. Admittedly, the Holy Spirit cannot be totally institutionalized in the sense that he is absorbed by structures. But he should not be falsely spiritualized either, especially by being torn apart from the church where the application of salvation takes place.

This rather strong emphasis on the church and the visible means of grace should not be taken to mean that the Spirit does not relate to or deal with us as individuals. On a personal level, the Holy Spirit brings about conversion, renewal, and participation in "the spirit of sonship" which makes us cry "Abba! Father!" (Rom. 8:15). But this does not imply that we are given over to shifting spiritual sensations. At this point, the task of the Spirit is to link the objective and the subjective aspects of faith together. And this is done not least of all through the sacraments, which — due to the Spirit's presence — are the key instruments of our personal participation in the fruits of Christ's offering at the cross.

The church is not the sole arena of the Holy Spirit, but it is his most crucial focus. On this basis, Whitsun — with its emphasis on the outpouring of the Spirit — is frequently identified as the church's birthday. This idea is understandable, but hardly correct. For the church is grounded in the work of the earthly Jesus and was, accordingly, a reality before the first Pentecost. Without the invigorating activity of the Spirit, the church would have been a rather lifeless entity. But without Jesus, there would have been no church at all. Yet, this sacred institution only stands forth in its full power and truth after the sending of the Spirit. This is affirmed and demonstrated in the Acts of the Apostles. Consequently, one might describe Whitsun as the baptism day of the church.

Finally, the Spirit who is the giver of life is concerned with all sides of our existence. God the Holy Spirit cannot be confined to a narrow spiritualized sphere. And in most cases, his dealing with us does not lead to our being taken away from daily life and the world. All forms of religious escapism and false heaven-flight are signs of a misplaced or spiritualized spirituality. The Holy Spirit is our breath of life. He is meant to be our shield and support when the world gets nasty. His fruits are associated with elementary human virtues. His work is anchored in empirically perceptible means — i.e., in things we can see and hear, taste and smell. He meets us in the space of the church and not in surreal experiences. And he equips us to live a truly spiritual life in and for the world, serving all creation. Along such lines, the Holy Spirit becomes the grounded wire of our Christian life and the solid foundation of our faith. This is also why he is able to provide an equally solid foundation for a materialist spirituality.

A vigorous and appropriate summary of the theology of the Holy Spirit can be found in the ancient hymn of the church, *Veni Creator Spiritus:*

> Come, Holy Ghost, Creator blest,
> and in our hearts take up Thy rest;
> come with Thy grace and heav'nly aid,
> To fill the hearts which Thou hast made.
>
> O Comforter, to Thee we cry,
> Thou heav'nly gift of God most high,
> Thou Fount of life, and Fire of love,
> and sweet anointing from above.
>
> O Finger of the hand divine,
> the sevenfold gifts of grace are thine;
> true promise of the Father thou,
> who dost the tongue with power endow.
>
> Thy light to every sense impart,
> and shed thy love in every heart;
> thine own unfailing might supply
> to strengthen our infirmity.
>
> Drive far away our ghostly foe,
> and thine abiding peace bestow;
> if thou be our preventing Guide,
> no evil can our steps betide.

> Praise we the Father and the Son
> and Holy Spirit with them One;
> and may the Son on us bestow
> the gifts that from the Spirit flow.

It is hardly possible to get farther away from a narrow and cramped focus on ecstatic sensations and private religious consumption than this. At the same time, the bonds between creation and redemption are made evident once more. The work of God the holy and creating Spirit starts in our "heart" — and in "every sense." But it points towards the day when the power of sin over creation shall cease and the world shall be redeemed. Seen in this perspective, the Holy Spirit also becomes the Spirit of comfort and hope for all who "(groan) in travail together" and long for the time when "creation itself will be set free from its bondage to decay and obtain the glorious liberty of the children of God" (Rom. 8:21-22). This is essential to a materialist spirituality.

Literature

Generally, there is much literature on the Holy Spirit today. A significant part of it appears to be practical manuals, describing in concrete steps how we can be "filled by the Spirit." Titles include *Good Morning, Holy Spirit; The Holy Spirit, My Senior Partner*, etc. Since my familiarity with such literature is clearly limited, I have not listed any of these titles below.

Burgess, Stanley, and Eduard van der Maas. *The New International Dictionary of Pentecostal and Charismatic Movements*, new edition. Grand Rapids: Zondervan, 2001.

Burge, Gary M., and I. Howard Marshall. *The Anointed Community: Holy Spirit in the Johannine Tradition*. Grand Rapids: Eerdmans, 1987.

Congar, Yves. *I Believe in the Holy Spirit*. New York: Crossroad, 1997.

Cordes, Paul Josef. *Call to Holiness: Reflections on the Catholic Charismatic Movement*. Collegeville, MN: Michael Glazier/Liturgical Press, 1997.

Csordas, Thomas J. *The Sacred Self: A Cultural Phenomenology of Charismatic Healing*, new edition. Berkeley: University of California Press, 1997.

Fee, Gordon D. *Paul, the Spirit, and the People of God*. Peabody, MA: Hendrickson, 2005.

O'Carroll, Michael. *Veni Creator Spiritus: Encyclopedia of the Holy Spirit.* Collegeville, MN: Michael Glazier/Liturgical Press, 1991.

Smail, Tom, Andrew Walker, and Nigel Wright. *The Love of Power or the Power of Love: A Careful Assessment of the Problem with the Charismatic and Word-of-Faith-Movements.* Minneapolis: Bethany House Publishers, 1994.

Suenens, Leon-Joseph. *A New Pentecost?* New York: Seabury Press, 1984.

Turner, Max. *The Holy Spirit and Spiritual Gifts: In the New Testament and Today.* Carlisle, UK: Paternoster Press, 1996.

CHURCH AND SACRAMENTS

6 The Church

Place of Salvation and Priest of Creation

I have already pointed out that Christian faith does not consist in subscribing to a more or less firmly defined set of ideas and beliefs. Faith is first and foremost life — a whole, full, and true life; the life God has envisioned for us. This life is not lived out within an abstract vacuum. As all sorts of life, it requires a space where it is born, shaped, and nourished. And this space is the church. Seen against this background, the church plays a key role in our life in Christ — not least as this life is depicted and realized within the framework of a materialist spirituality. While the Holy Spirit is the breath of our Christian life, the church provides its indispensable breathing environment. It is, thus, the place of salvation.

This, however, does not happen detached from or in opposition to God's creation. I repeat: Church and world are clearly interconnected. And the church's aim is not only the saving of souls, but the redemption of creation. It is, therefore, both the place of salvation and the priest of creation. These two aspects of its sending and service must not be separated. In the church seemingly contrary elements are held together, on the basis of the incarnation: the divine and true humanity, heaven and earth, redemption and creation. Accordingly, the church must be explored from "below" as well as from "above." And its identity is defined by two interrelated focal points: its sacramentally anchored communion and its mission in and for the world.

In exploring ecclesiology further, we must distinguish between the spiritual nature of the church and its institutional aspects. The main point is what fills the church, its contents. Yet, these aspects cannot be torn apart. For both the institution and the church building are essential. Without them there can be no church in the full meaning of the term. The institution as well as the building has crucial ecclesiological significance. This is due to the fact that the gifts we receive in the church do not float around freely; they are only available in a specific space or an equally specific room. Moreover, this space is not totally silent or an empty set-piece. Quite on the contrary, it offers an important specification and deepening of the church's content-side. Thus seen, architecture becomes theology. And the physical church building is more than a void shell. It is the place for our encounter with Christ, he who comes to us as a human being.

In the previous chapter, we have seen that Paul thinks very concretely when he describes the church as the body of Christ. This concept does not only apply to successful congregations or the church at its best. According to 1 Corinthians 12, the body of Christ can be found wherever Christ is present with the salvation he bestows. And this act is not connected with abstract ideas, but takes place through externally visible means — especially God's word and the sacraments. These means constitute or so to speak create the church.

This particularly applies to the Eucharist. In the sacrament of the altar, Christ's sacrifice at the cross and its fruits are made concretely present among us. Here salvation becomes ours. And here the church's nature as the body of Christ is expressed in a very direct way: "The cup of blessing which we bless, is it not a participation in the blood of Christ? The bread which we break, is it not a participation in the body of Christ? Because there is one bread, we who are many are one body, for we all partake of the one bread" (1 Cor. 10:16-17). This means that the church becomes the body of Christ when we together eat the one bread, the bread that is Christ. Seen in this perspective, the Eucharist makes the church and should be perceived as its central icon.

All this shows that the church, which is Christ's body on earth, cannot be without significance in the communication of salvation. It is rather the space where our faith life is initiated through baptism; it is the mother of faith. But since we here share in the fruits of the Calvary event, it is also the place of salvation. This corresponds with the assertion of St. Cyprian that we cannot have God as father unless we have the church as mother. In the church Christ's sacrifice lives on — not as an abstract notion or a pious idea, but as a sacramental reality. Surely, the ecclesial institution cannot save anyone; Christ is the only way to salvation. But he is present as savior in a concrete and visible space. This is a vital part of the gospel of grace. For grace too is no abstract idea. It exists and is mediated in a place that people can relate to through their senses.

This is the chief reason why the visibility of the church is so important. What is at stake here is not high-church fancies or an exaggerated concern for structures. The point is simply that people shall be able to *see* the church, and thus seek and receive the salvation that is offered to all within its walls through word and sacrament. This suggests that visibility pertains to the accessibility of grace and the "democratization" of faith, being grounded in elementary empirical perception. It is within such a context that the visible nature of the church becomes essential to its life and mission.

In the wake of this, we acknowledge that the church cannot be reduced to the level of pure abstraction. Also in its capacity as a spiritual reality, it is always attached to a specific institutional framework, tangible structures, and a concrete space. On the one hand, ecclesial structures are marked by a certain ambivalence in the sense that they can reflect God's grace but also disturbing examples of human sinfulness. On the other hand, this does not signify that the presence of Jesus within these structures is annulled. For the Christ who became a human being like us can also make room for himself and be present in and through partly human structures. In the same way as he was incarnated in the flesh, he is today incarnated within a church that carries human features. Here it should be noted that the church as such is not a part of the incarnation act; it is rather the space for Christ's continual incarnation. This is the reason why our prayer *Agnus Dei* — "Lamb of God" — is not only directed to the heavenly Son of God, but also to Christ at the altar — he who is so close to us that he can be eaten and drunk in and through the bread and the wine of the Eucharist.

The intention of this strong emphasis on the place and role of the church is definitely not to say that salvation is exclusively available within the Roman ecclesial institution. Now, the Dogmatic Constitution on the Church of the Second Vatican Council underscores that the true church of Christ exists — or subsists — within this institution. But this does not mean that other churches are seen as invalid or empty. For

73

the Council's Decree on Ecumenism states that these churches and communities are effective instruments in the mediation of salvation in Christ through the Holy Spirit. And — most importantly: God is omnipotent; he saves whoever he will when and where he will. This also suggests that salvation outside the ecclesial institution is a possibility. Or — more precisely: The church may have a far greater range than we think. Yet, we are not God. And in our case the normal rule applies: Salvation is available within the space of the church. This is crucial to our service and mission in the world.

The biblical witness to the church is the crucial point of departure for ecclesiology. The "body of Christ" is a highly important concept in this witness (cf. especially 1 Cor. 12; Rom. 12; and Eph. 4). We have already noted that this term implies a concrete interrelatedness between Christ and the church which is his body on earth. Another essential concept is the description of the church as "the people of God" (cf. *inter alia* Rom. 9:25-26; 2 Cor. 6:16; and Titus 2:14). Here the dynamic nature of the church as a pilgrim people and its continuity with the people of Israel are underlined. Through various notions, the close interconnection between the church and the Holy Spirit is expressed: It is a "dwelling place of God in the Spirit" (Eph. 2:20) and a "spiritual house" or a temple of the Spirit (cf. 1 Peter 2:4-5). Taken together, these concepts reflect the Trinitarian foundation of the church.

In the New Testament, the church is also pictured as *koinonia* or *communio* — accentuating its vertical as well as its horizontal anchoring: ". . . that which we have seen and heard we proclaim also to you, so that you may have fellowship *(koinonia)* with us; and our fellowship *(koinonia)* is with the Father and with his Son Jesus Christ" (1 John 1:3). This *koinonia* is actually more than a "fellowship," it signifies our specific and concrete participation with the Father through the Son in the Spirit. Additionally, the church is a worshiping and sacramental community (cf. *inter alia* 1 Cor. 11 and 14); it is "the pillar and bulwark of the truth" (1 Tim. 3:15); it is sent to the world with a message and a mission (cf. Matt. 28:18-20); it is a community of sharing and solidarity (cf. Acts 2:42-47); and it is eschatologically directed — pointing towards the fulfillment of God's kingdom (cf. 1 and 2 Thess.).

Seen in this light, the claims that the Bible has no ecclesiology must be rejected. On the contrary, the New Testament offers a rich vision of the church that is still binding as well as momentous. Yet, it must be realized that the church is a living entity — not least in the sense that it is and has to be marked by historical change. The New Testament reflects shifts in the church's life when it is confronted with fresh challenges. In the account of Peter's mission among non-Jews in Acts 10 and 11, we note that the Spirit so to speak enforces a new openness towards other people. Additional changes stem from the fact that a growing and in due course multi-national church had different needs than the small apostolically led congregations of the first Christians.

The establishment of an initially local and then regional ministry of episcopal oversight — in keeping with the principle of one bishop in each city, is an example of this. At a later stage, the need for structures of oversight at the universal level became evident — pointing towards the basic intention of the ministry of the Bishop of Rome. In general terms, the church is characterized by a dynamic development. And this development is echoed in its tradition as a whole. One-dimensional fundamentalism is, therefore, perhaps even more unhelpful in the field of ecclesiology than in other parts of theology.

The New Testament ecclesiological legacy is implicitly summarized in the Nicene Creed's listing of four basic marks or attributes of the one church of Christ — unity, holiness, catholicity, and apostolicity. These marks have the following implications: Unity belongs to the church's nature and cannot be reduced to an optional extra in its life. The holiness of the church stems from God's holiness and can only on that basis be perceived as a moral quality. Catholicity points to the church's existence across time and space. Apostolicity connects the church to the apostolic witness to Christ and thus provides it with an authoritative foundation. All the four ecclesial marks are interrelated.

In this and the next chapters, different aspects of the ecclesiological position that have been indicated so far will be further investigated. Here the focus is on the fundamental nature of the church and its implications. In chapter 6, the means of grace and sacramentality will be explored. And in chapter 7, worship life and liturgy are at the core. The goal of these deliberations is not to present a complete view of the church; I hope to be able to do that in another volume on ecumenical ecclesiology. In this connection, the key concern is the church's role in our spiritual life, with an emphasis on a materialist spirituality. Before I look more closely at this, however, something must be said about the negative background of my position — or about currents that are ecclesiologically counterproductive. Such currents have been quite plentiful in Norway, which is the main context of my deliberations. But they can also be traced elsewhere.

The twentieth century has been referred to as the age of the church. This may have been the case in earlier stages. But towards the end of the century and at the dawn of the new millennium, the concern for ecclesiology has decreased — among theologians as well as the faithful. Within Protestantism the church institution has hardly ever been essential. This is partly due to a misconception of the ecclesiology of the Lutheran reformation. While the reformers could describe the church as "hidden" in the sense that only God knew its true members, this was later confused with the idea that the church was invisible according to its nature. Such an opinion fitted nicely to the accentuation of the personal or individual character of religion within the Protestant tradition. Here the church was at best considered as a purely practical institution, at worst as a direct impediment of true personalized faith — also minimizing the role of the sacraments. The result was a largely church-less religion of the heart.

Pietism and so-called liberal theology depart on several points. In regard to ecclesiology, however, these two currents often emerge as one of a kind. For the question whether faith should be anchored in the heart, as Pietists claim, or in the mind, in accordance with the favored liberal solution, is only of theoretical importance since both these movements distance themselves from an ecclesially grounded faith. Lately, we have witnessed an increasing tendency to fuse Pietism and liberalism into a kind of Liberal-Pietism — especially on the basis of a shared approach to the church. This alliance can be highly influential and contributes effectively to the decline in ecclesiological awareness.

One consequence of Liberal-Pietism is the steady growth of privatized religion. People still believe, but they believe in their own manner. A commonly binding religious life is marginalized, while churches that dare to interfere in how we construct our private beliefs are confronted with hefty complaints: No one is entitled to meddle with *my* religion! This explains why it is so hard to exercise ecclesial authority today. Priests are trumped by jabbering celebrities who deliver incredibly shallow answers to the great questions of life. In this situation, there is a desperate need for effective spiritual leadership. We need shepherds who can help us to draw from the riches of the church's faith treasure and to abstain from a vain religious reinvention of the wheel.

As a result of privatization, many are eager to do what a Norwegian rock-star-pastor recommends — namely to occupy the backbench of the church. Now, seen from one point of view there is nothing wrong with these benches — since the last shall become the first. But the backbench syndrome should not be turned into a key religious principle that entices people to sneak out without having moved cautiously closer to the front in order to experience what happens at the altar. Today it has become a self-fulfilling prophecy that everything is so dreadfully boring in the church. And quite a few would like to instruct us on how things could be more thrilling when God's people gather. Here it seems to be a common attitude that "Jesus is okay, but the church is hopeless" — as if Christ can be torn apart from the church that is his body on earth.

Within the churches, many try desperately to meet such challenges by measures that are put forth as "renewal." There can be no doubt that the church needs renewal. However, the renewal campaigns tend to force us into a relentless pursuit of ever stronger and more bizarre experiences. These campaigns are designed to compete with a huge number of TV channels that make it possible to watch the most shocking events in the midst of our living rooms. The church can never succeed in such a competition. We will only end up with unbearable noise or lukewarm leisurely entertainment. A better approach would be to allow the church to stand forth as it is meant to be, i.e., radically different. But we do not quite dare to take such a step; instead we put our stakes on the exhausting loudness or superficial coziness that is on bid everywhere.

Okay, now my pressure has been relieved — now it is due time to turn to something I hope will be more constructive. Do not misunderstand me; I do not want to mock well-meant efforts at renewal. I fully appreciate the desperate feeling of having to watch people disappearing from the church. The challenges we face in this field are complicated and cannot be addressed through simple solutions — neither mine nor those of others. And I sympathize with open-minded attempts to explore new proposals for a functioning spirituality — be it along the lines of the charismatic movement or currents with premodern features.

However, as the Norwegian author Alexander Kielland phrased it: When there is a fire, you do not whisper — you scream! My perhaps frantic shout goes like this: Steer away from market-sensitive flamboyance; abstain from futile attempts to reinvent the wheel; leave noise and gaudiness behind — and let the church be the church. This may be the most appropriate measure in identifying a viable renewal for the Christian communities. For a church that neglects the maintaining of true identity is bound to degenerate.

On this basis, I have to admit that I harbor grave doubts about a large portion of the renewal schemes. And I get agitated when renewal-prophets line up with their kitschy commodities and cheap solutions. Why? Because people are being offered stones instead of bread. This is an inevitable outcome when access to the rich faith deposit of the church is barred. Let me add that it grieves me when people plop down on the backbenches in the church — and stay there. My appeal to all those who keep the church at arm's length is, therefore, like this: Come in! Move forward! And see that the church, despite its lacks and short-comings, is the place of salvation.

How, then, can a healthy ecclesiological consciousness be promoted? What is the best way out of the present deadlock in this field? Obviously, I cannot answer these complicated questions on my own. But I have some suggestions:

The first one is that we must try to demonstrate the strength and sheer joy of believing together, as communion. Despite the present drift towards privatization in all sectors of society, human beings are created for fellowship. This also applies to our life in Christ. We have already noted how the early church argued that a single Christian can hardly be a Christian. Instead, it was strongly emphasized that we believe as a community or as a body. Within the body of the church, apostolic ministries grew forth that had a special if not exclusive responsibility to interpret, develop, and defend the faith. An important aspect of this was to prevent individuals or groups from annexing what belonged to everyone. The fact that a special theological and spiritual responsibility was attributed to the ministries was rarely seen as a limitation, but rather as a help — not least in times of persecution. Generally, the ecclesial body would be in a disastrous shape without a head. This head is primarily Christ, but also those who are entrusted with apostolic leadership. Yet, a head that disregards the body is a poor alternative here. This actualizes the crucial interaction between leadership and people within the church — or its communal character.

The fact that we believe together does not exclude an awareness of the personal aspects of Christian life. Our faith must somehow be grounded in our personality and requires personal commitment. Without such commitment, we may end up with a more or less dead faith. But faith is not a purely individual concern, let alone a private thing. Quite the contrary; like love, our shared faith binds us together in a mutually committed fellowship. This is the framework of our life in Christ as well as our witness to the world. Accordingly, faith must be personally anchored — but it can never be a private entity.

I shall return to the collective aspects of our faith life in chapter 12. Here I will settle with briefly indicating one vital point: The church cannot believe on our behalf. But it can teach us what it means to have a Christian faith, it can enrich our interpretation of the truths of faith, and it can supply and fulfill our faith — especially in times of doubt and tribulation. This is why the Roman Catholic Church in the liturgy of the Mass prays with the following words: "Look not on our sins, but on the faith of your Church, and grant us the peace and unity of your Kingdom, where you live forever and ever." And we respond: Amen, in gratitude to the church that is the mother of faith and that can complete our often frail and lacking faith. In my case, I do not see how I could manage without this. And I want to share the reassurance it gives with everybody.

Second, in the wake of this — or rather as a part of it — the church emerges as a community of care, compassion, and solidarity. In spite of the privatization-wave, this is what we long for. Not least in the Eucharistic celebration, there is a strong connection between praying together and the sharing of temporal goods. The Eucharist is not only the sacrament of the altar, but also a communion meal and a foretaste of the heavenly meal. This had clear consequences for the first Christians: ". . . all who believed were together and had all things in common; and they sold their possessions and goods and distributed them to all, as any had need. And day by day, attending the temple together and breaking the bread in their homes, they partook of food with glad and generous hearts, praising God and having favor with all the people . . ." (Acts 2:44-47). Furthermore: "When you meet together, it is not the

Lord's supper that you eat. For in eating, each one goes ahead with his own meal, and one is hungry and another is drunk. What! Do you not have houses to eat and drink in? Or do you despise the church of God and humiliate those who have nothing?" (1 Cor. 11:20-22).

These concerns are not only meant as internal ideals, but apply to the church's service in the world. Especially in a context where a huge and growing number of people desperately lack what they need for their daily lives and where poverty is spreading also in affluent societies, we are obliged to share our bread with others. Such sharing is integral to the nature and mission of the church. It also functions as a forceful critical corrective over against both "the theology of prosperity" and the internal preoccupation that marks quite a few congregations. The insistence that a human tends to be *incurvatus in se* — turned or curved inward on oneself — ranks among the most essential parts of the legacy of Martin Luther. This observation is anthropologically, socially, and ecclesiologically valid. When we describe the church as a community of love and solidarity, it is also meant as a remedial to attitudes like this — aiming at a restoration of the mutual care and compassion that God intended for his creation.

Third, I have already briefly indicated that the church is construed as an effective sign of the kingdom of God. This is grounded in its sacramental nature. But it also has social and moral implications. According to the gospel, God's kingdom is a place where the smallest are the greatest, the last become the first, and children are seen as role models. This is totally different from the societies we have formed, not least in their market-fundamentalist shape. But it is in full correspondence with God's good will for his creation.

The church emerges as a forceful critical corrective over against destructive features in our society. This takes place through its sheer presence as a sign of the kingdom, without assuming a bluntly political or politicized role. Moreover, the inclusive nature of the church becomes evident in its capacity as a foretaste of God's kingdom. Here there is ample space for the smallest among us. The church that is a sign of the kingdom is also directed towards its eschatological goal, without departing from the world. This is yet another example of how heaven and earth are kept together.

Fourth, the church provides the main framework for an unfolding of our faith's rich diversity and abundance. Basically, there is not so much that *must* be believed in the church. But there is much that *can* and *should* be believed, simply because it will make our Christian life significantly richer. Obviously, the church's faith deposit has a core — being identical with Christ, he who is the cornerstone and the only foundation we can build on. Yet, this conviction should not be used as a remedy to cut off things from our faith treasure, but rather as a means that enables us to understand, handle, and rejoice in the fullness of this treasure. Thus seen, our diverse and profuse tradition is a gift — and not a threat. Behind this diversity stands a huge crowd of witnesses, across time as well as space.

In some Protestant circles there has been a tendency to identify an increasingly narrow center of faith. There has also been an inclination to play out this center against faith's breadth and comprehensiveness. This particularly applies to some interpretations of the principles "Scripture (or word) alone," "faith alone," and "grace alone." I would contest such interpretations. *Sola scriptura* should actually be translated "*by* Scripture alone" — seeing the biblical witness as a hermeneutical core in the universe of faith. Moreover, faith is actually never "alone"; it should always be accompanied by good works. And grace does not exclude the transforming power of Christ's work *in* us as human beings. Generally, I have problems in seeing these vital principles associated with the barren and narrow adverb "alone" — at least if it blocks our access to the wealth of our tradition. In the world of faith, things are connected. And the central Christian truths should not be placed in a vacuum; they are always the center of *something*. And this "something" contributes significantly to our growth in faith.

Sterile reductionism or minimalism is probably a key reason why neo-religious groups and noisy charismatics have been able to sell their rather shallow stuff so efficiently. When the abundance of the church's tradition is suppressed or neglected, there is a clear danger that people are being offered — and are prone to accept — stones instead of bread. Hence, the best way to face and counteract ostentatious market spiritualities may be to put our stakes on and trust in the plentiful but somewhat more sober richness of our faith treasure. Here the challenge is not to focus on as little as possible, but rather to share this treasure in its fullness. This may prevent people from choosing shallowness in flamboyant wrappings. If we at the same time manage to stay clear of retrospective nostalgia, this is a feasible way towards true renewal.

Fifth, our faith is concretized and visualized in the space of the church. This deviates from the idea often entertained today, that religion is supposed to be an inward and largely invisible entity. Yet, I assume many share my experience that such religiosity is hard to integrate and practice in our hectic and fluctuating lives. We need something more palpable, something that does not require a spiritual concentration that only a minority is able to produce; something that transcends the inward piety of the heart. And quite a few of us have realized that it is somehow better to relate to a concrete space and a specific practice than to abstract notions and internalized beliefs. The concretization of faith is first and foremost connected with the word and the sacraments. But the liturgy, ritual acts, and a comprehensive sign language play important roles here, too. And all these things are located in the space of the church.

Admittedly, there is a tension between what is readily visible and what remains unseen in the Christian faith. I shall return to this tension later on. But already at this stage, some basic concerns must be recorded: We believe in a Triune God in whom the Father is the creator, the Son became flesh, and the Spirit works through empirically perceptible means. Since God, therefore, is no abstract principle, our faith in God cannot be grounded in abstract principles either. Furthermore, several of the invisible realities of faith are revealed to us in Christ — if in a preliminary way. And finally, the ambiguity of faith that is caused by the tension between visibility and invisibility is transcended within the church. Here we envision as in a mirror what we eventually shall see face to face.

In light of points like these, one would hope that a new ecclesiological awareness can be established. They show that the church is more than a mere practical framework of an internalized religiosity — and it is definitely not an impediment to authentic faith. It is rather the body of Christ, "the fullness of him who fills all in all" (Eph. 2:23). It is thus the mother of faith; it is the place of salvation; it is the space where we participate in and benefit from Christ's sacrifice; it is the caring and inclusive community of faith; and it is the priest of creation. This simply implies that the church is clearly helpful and beneficial; it may even be indispensable to faith. I shall not maintain that it is totally impossible for Christians to manage without the church. But based on my own experiences, I am prone to suggest that those who try this will do themselves a spiritual disservice of enormous proportions.

What I have said so far points towards and contributes significantly to a materialist spirituality. Such spirituality is sacramentally grounded and ecclesially framed — i.e., a piety that is attached to the visible church and its sacramental foundation, and is confident that the church is the place where Jesus Christ meets us in a highly real way and offers us our share in the gifts of salvation. It must be underlined, though, that this does not exclude an awareness of and a grief over the sad fact that the church has failed in the past and will continue to do so in the future. Within this entity, divine realities and human failures will persist side by side until Christ returns in order to fulfill his work. Accordingly, true church piety is also characterized by unyielding realism — in the sense that it focuses on the factual shape of the church and not on a distant ideal. This further shows that a materialist spirituality is fully aware that all ecclesial institutions require constructive criticism. And it realizes that the church is called to penance and continual conversion. Here I would like to quote Gertrud von Le Fort with consent: *Wer an die Kirche nicht leidet, liebt sie nicht* — the one who does not suffer over the church, does not love it.

Simultaneously, it is actually the church which never can escape from its failures that is the mother of faith and the place of salvation — it is even a potential pillar of truth. But this does not depend on its own achievements and qualities. The crucial role of the church in the drama of salvation is anchored in the fact that God is capable of equipping and sustaining it through his gracious gifts in the Holy Spirit. Moreover, when Paul describes the church as the body of Christ in a very real manner, it cannot be understood as an award for steadfast and heroic faith. The point is rather that as long as Christ is concretely present within it, it remains his visible body on earth — and thus the unwavering *sacrament of salvation*. This is confirmed through God's steadfast promise to the church that the gates of hell shall never prevail over it.

Everyone who looks for a perfect church will be seriously disappointed. Still, this community is the bearer of an immense potential, regardless of its faults and powerlessness. This conviction is firmly anchored in an experience that has accompanied the church from its beginning — namely that God can transform weak and timid members of the body of Christ into bold and fierce witnesses to the gospel. At the final instance, this is a feature of the church's life just as evident as its obvious lacks — since God never fails his children.

An accurate and constructive expression of this position can be found in the Porvoo Common Statement from the dialogue between Anglicans and Lutherans in Northern Europe. I quote paragraph 20 of the statement:

> The Church is a divine reality, holy and transcending present finite reality; at the same time, as a human institution, it shares the brokenness of human community in its ambiguity and frailty. The Church is always called to repentance, reform and renewal, and has constantly to depend on God's mercy and forgiveness. The Scriptures offer a portrait of a Church living in the light of the Gospel:
>
> – it is a Church rooted and grounded in the love and grace of the Lord Christ;
> – it is a Church always joyful, praying continually and giving thanks even in the midst of suffering;
> – it is a pilgrim Church, a people of God with a new heavenly citizenship, a holy nation and a royal priesthood;
> – it is a Church which makes common confession of the apostolic faith in word and in life, the faith common to the whole Church everywhere and at all times;
> – it is a Church with a mission to all in every race and nation, preaching the gospel, proclaiming the forgiveness of sins, baptizing and celebrating the eucharist;
> – it is a Church which is served by an ordained apostolic ministry, sent by God to gather and nourish the people of God in each place, uniting and linking them with the Church universal within the whole communion of saints;
> – it is a Church which manifests through its visible communion the healing and uniting power of God amidst the divisions of humankind;
> – it is a Church in which the bonds of communion are strong enough to enable it to bear effective witness in the world, to guard and interpret the apostolic faith, to take decisions, to teach authoritatively, and to share its goods with those in need;
> – it is a Church alive and responsive to the hope which God has set before it, to the wealth and glory of the share God has offered it in the heritage of his people, and to the vastness of the resources of God's power open to those who trust in him.

This portrait of the Church is by no means complete; nevertheless, it confronts our churches with challenges to the fidelity of our lives and with a constant need for repentance and renewal.

(Conversations between the British and Irish Anglican Churches and the Nordic and Baltic Lutheran Churches: The Porvoo Common Statement, 1992)

In this account, several additional features that are essential to a materialist spirituality are emphasized: The church is sent to the world in order to safeguard creation, to protect everything that is truly human, to carry the burdens of the suffering, to fight against oppression, and to serve as a sign of unity in a broken world. In this way, the Porvoo Statement affirms that the church's nature as the place of salvation and its calling as the priest of creation are clearly interrelated.

Some argue that the image of the church presented in the Porvoo text is idealistic and a bit naïve. However, this portrait is anchored in the vision of the church outlined in Holy Scripture. This is what we strive for and aim at. I appreciate that it has not been fully accomplished. But there is no law that implies that such a vision takes us beyond all conceivable reality — particularly not for a church that is committed to and firmly set on God's calling. At any rate, the shortcomings of the church may conceal its beauty. Yet, this beauty is never terminated. For the church remains the place where the most beautiful thing that can be imagined is celebrated and sacramentally represented — namely the one who gives his life for the many.

Literature

Henn, William. *Church: The People of God.* London: Burns & Oates/Continuum, 2004.

Lathrop, Gordon W. *Holy People: A Liturgical Ecclesiology.* Minneapolis: Fortress, 1999.

Mannion, Gerard. *Ecclesiology and Postmodernity: Questions for the Church in Our Time.* Collegeville, MN: Michael Glazier/Liturgical Press, 2007.

Martini, Carlo Cardinal. *Reflections on the Church: Meditations on Vatican II.* Dublin: Veritas, 1987.

McPartlan, Paul. *Sacrament of Salvation: Introduction to Eucharistic Ecclesiology.* London: T. & T. Clark/Continuum, 1995.

Moltmann, Jürgen. *The Church in the Power of the Spirit: A Contribution to Messianic Ecclesiology.* Minneapolis: Augsburg/Fortress, 1993.

Ratzinger, Joseph. *Called to Communion: Understanding the Church Today,* 3rd revised edition. Fort Collins, CO: Ignatius Press, 1996.

Rausch, Thomas P. *Towards a Truly Catholic Church: An Ecclesiology for the Third Millennium.* Collegeville, MN: Michael Glazier/Liturgical Press, 2003.

Schnackenburg, Rudolf. *The Church in the New Testament.* London: Burns & Oates, 1965.

Zizioulas, John. *Being as Communion: Studies in Personhood and the Church,* new edition. Crestwood, NY: St. Vladimir's Seminary Press, 1993.

7 Sacraments and Sacramentality

The Backbone of Our Life in Christ

The sacraments are often referred to as visible signs of God's invisible grace. This definition has its roots in St. Augustine and emphasizes a vital aspect of the nature of the sacraments. At the same time, it must be underlined that the sacramental acts primarily aim at rescuing grace from a vague and unclear sphere of abstract ideas — or from the spiritualized ivory tower where it occasionally has been located. When we share in the sacraments, grace is not invisible anymore. Then it can actually be seen and heard; it can even be eaten and drunk in the Eucharist. This explains why the sacraments and sacramentality on the whole play a central role in a materialist spirituality. Such spirituality emerges as a sacramental spirituality, e.g., as a piety where the sacraments provide a red thread from the beginning of our life till its end.

As compared to flamboyant market spiritualities, the sacraments have a rather ordinary appearance — insisting that God's grace is mediated through basic elements from creation like water, bread, and wine. This is probably a key reason why the prophets of ferocious renewal tend to ignore sacramentality. Yet, the strength of their plain character is that sacramental grace is available to everyone through common empirical sensation. Moreover, the concreteness of the sacramental acts points towards their effectiveness. Despite a humble exterior, the sacraments are fully capable of delivering what they pledge. Baptism is participation in Christ's death and resurrection, the Eucharist does make us members of the body of Christ, and confession really mediates forgiveness.

In the wake of this, sacramental grace comes across as *transforming grace*. Here salvation is offered to us freely, as a gift. But when we share in the fruits of Christ's sacrifice, our lives are also transformed in the sense that we grow towards what God the creator intended us to be. And this growth does not only apply to us as individuals. It has specific implications in view of our relationship to our fellow human beings as well as creation as a whole. Thus seen, transforming sacramental grace has moral and social consequences.

Particularly on the Lutheran side, the sacraments — together with God's word or the promise of the gospel — are characterized as means of grace. Basically, this concept is parallel to key aspects in Catholic sacramental theology. It implies that our partaking in grace in Christ occurs through outward, concrete, and effective signs. Grace is no mere idea; it does not float around in a vacuum. It is mediated through things we can see, hear, and relate to through our senses. On this background, the means of grace — i.e., the word and the sacraments — can be described as the backbone of our life in Christ.

The relationship between word and sacrament has been explained somewhat differently by Lutherans and Catholics. In Lutheran theology, the word is the point of departure that takes its shape in the sacraments. On the Catholic side, the word is attributed with a sacramental character. Here, however, the sequence is less important. The chief concern is the dialectic or interconnection between word and sacrament. On the one hand, God's promise in Christ is at the core of the sacramental acts. On the other hand, a sacrament can be understood as *verbum visibile* — a "visible word." It therefore becomes senseless to play word and sacrament out against each other.

When God reveals himself, a living person — Jesus Christ — is at the core. In the Johannine writings, Jesus is described as the Word, the *logos* of God. This means that the word does not only provide us with information; it actually embraces and effectively mediates Jesus. And this applies to the external word, the word that is read and heard in our worship service. Here we find the basis of the word's status as a means of grace. In this capacity, the word also constitutes the center of God's revelation. Accordingly, all types of revelation must be approached and assessed with Christ, God's living word, as lens.

In more practical terms, God's revelation is essentially attached to

Holy Scripture, without being identical with the Bible. God reveals himself in many ways — in his creation, in the hearts of human beings and, above all, in the church. It must be emphasized, though, that this revelation never takes place in blatant opposition to what is stated in God's word to us as expressed in Scripture. Accordingly, the Bible becomes the key criterion of revelation; it becomes the foundation of our efforts to distinguish between true and false revelation and to "try the spirits." As far as I can gather, this corresponds with vital aspects of the Lutheran principle *sola scriptura* — or *by* Scripture alone. This principle does not mean that the Bible is left in a lonely vacuum, but rather that it is perceived as the center of the church's faith treasure or of its tradition. Church tradition should, therefore, be read in light of the scriptures. Seen in this perspective, revelation may have two — or more — sources. But Holy Scripture always remains at the core when God reveals himself.

Admittedly, "Scripture alone" is interpreted in different ways. During the last decades, a pietistically inclined "word alone" rhetoric — suggesting that there is the word of God and little or nothing else — has had a renaissance, not least in ecumenically related conflicts. Within the framework of a linguistically directed, typically postmodern, and in practice similar approach, there is an inclination to insist that the word became — not flesh, but "text." This is frequently coupled with excessive use of the fashionable term "story." As a Catholic, I am uncomfortable with the "word alone" position; I would even argue that it departs from authentic Reformation theology on crucial points.

Generally, it must be underscored that all forms of biblical fundamentalism or so-called biblicism emerge as dead-ends. Such attitudes are incapable of grasping the breadth and richness of both revelation and the tradition of the church. Fundamentalism fails to account for the fact that God's word is a living and dynamic entity that speaks into ever new and changing contexts. The paradox of biblicism is that an approach aimed at securing the proper place of and commitment to God's word in practice is at risk of doing the opposite, i.e., of isolating and marginalizing this word. There is therefore a need to abstain from all types of static and counterproductive fundamentalism.

The gospel, as manifested in the apostolic witness to Christ, is the core of the word of God. As already indicated, this implies that the Bible always must be read in light of this core. Here, however, the point is not subtle interpretation acrobatics, but rather the opposite. The gospel is anchored in basic observations, namely in things the disciples saw, heard, and experienced in their life together with Jesus: "That which was from the beginning, which we have heard, which we have seen with our eyes, which we have looked at and our hands have touched — this we proclaim concerning the word of life" (1 John 1:1). When the gospel mediates participation in Christ and, therefore, in salvation, it depends on the fact that it implies a concrete encounter with Jesus through this "story."

Not least in this sense, the word can be characterized as an effective and dynamic means of grace: ". . . the word of God is living and active, sharper than any two-edged sword, piercing to the division of soul and spirit, of joints and marrow, and discerning the thoughts and intentions of the heart" (Heb. 4:12). Or to express it through a fundamental affirmation in a hymn by N. F. S. Grundtvig: It is a word that "creates what it names." Furthermore, what is at stake here is not an inner, spiritually interpreted word — let alone a secluded "text," but what Martin Luther referred to as the outward word, a word that is read and heard. Its core is not abstract ideas, but concrete events and acts.

Even if the gospel is the center of God's word, it is not its sole content. The word also includes the law of God — or his will for our lives and creation as a whole. Surely, no one can be saved by the law or through obedience to the law; that is just as impossible as attempts to lift oneself by the hair. Yet, the law also reveals God's good will, and therefore provides us with invaluable insights into how a true human and Christian life should be lived. In this sense, parts of the law remain obligatory to us. However, this obligation should not be seen as a heavy yoke, but rather as a gift. This depends on the fact that the law makes us familiar with the good ordinances and boundaries that the creator has set for our life in the world. Accordingly, God's word is not only relevant in view of our own personal salvation, but also as concerns our responsibility for all our fellow human beings and creation as a whole, while it longs for redemption in Christ.

When works of the law are produced in order to earn salvation, the law becomes a way to severe enslavement. The gospel of Christ is the only thing that can set us free from this slavery. The spiritual freedom that stems from the gospel is fundamental to a materialist spirituality. It must be realized, though, that there is a limit to how much freedom human beings can manage: "'All things are lawful for me,' but not all things are helpful" (1 Cor. 6:12). Further, "take care lest this liberty of yours somehow become a stumbling block to the weak" (1 Cor. 8:9). We should, therefore, join in a prayer formulated by the Catholic Swedish author Torgny Lindgren in one of his novels: ". . . grant our thoughts as much freedom as they can sustain."

The concrete distinction between law and gospel cannot be handled on a theoretical or abstract level. The question is rather how the word of God works — or "hits" — in different situations. Jesus' teaching on wealth and poverty offers an example here — largely being law to the rich, but gospel to the poor. This demonstrates that we cannot "control" God's word. It is a vivid and dynamic entity that is always capable of opening up new perspectives for us.

What has been said above affirms that the word of God is indispensable to Christian piety. This also applies to a materialist spirituality. The word plays an essential role in revelation as well as the mediation of salvation; it shows us how we shall live in the church and the world; and it exposes an extraordinary richness and dynamic. The psalmist is therefore correct: "Thy word is a lamp to my feet and a light to my path" (Ps. 119:105).

A sacrament cannot be understood merely as a ritual act — especially so in a situation where even our rituals are privatized. It consists of two things — God's promise as grounded in the gospel, and a so-called element or a material sign. The key signs are the water of baptism, the bread and wine of the Eucharist, and the oil for anointing of the sick. The laying on of hands in the sacrament of reconciliation or penance, confirmation, marriage, and ordination or holy orders is a vital sacramental sign, too — in analogy with expressions of true human love and as a symbol of continuity. As already pointed out, the promise and the sign should neither be mixed together nor torn apart. God's promise in Christ is at the core of the sacrament. But this promise is only fulfilled in connection with the outward element. This implies that the grace of baptism is available through water, the gifts of the Eucharist become ours through bread and wine, and God's healing power is mediated through the consecrated oil. In my opinion, this point cannot be stressed strongly enough. It explains why the sacraments are of crucial importance in our Christian life.

The sacramental signs are not distinguished by dense symbolism or soaring spirituality. These signs are basic items from creation — such as bread and wine, water and oil. God has chosen to attach his grace in Christ to such things. At the same time, the earthly elements include the world in the sacraments by effectively representing it — particularly in the Eucharist. Moreover, their concrete nature makes them available to empirical perception. There is thus no need for an inner disposition or special religious sensation in our sacramental celebration. "O taste and see that the Lord is good," we read in Psalm 34:8. And this is precisely what happens when water is dispersed on a child in baptism, when the priest's hand is laid on our head in confirmation, and when we "eat" Christ in the Eucharist. Here the invisible aspects of our faith life are transcended; here what no eye has seen becomes visible to all; here heaven and earth meet. These concerns must be kept in mind when the concept of sacrament is referred to as a *mysterion:* The connotation of this term is not a foggy mystery, but the opposite — namely a highly concrete sacramental act.

Seen in this way, the sacraments can be understood neither as more or less floating symbols nor as mere human acts of confession. They are true expressions of the saving action of God and, accordingly, real means of grace. Their efficacy does not depend on external factors like our spiritual disposition or the status of the priest, but on God's steadfast promise. This does not mean that the sacraments work, as it were, automatically. The many gifts they mediate are received and become ours through faith. However, this faith is never our own achievement. It is rather given to us and created in us — almost as a creation out of nothing, a *creatio ex nihilo* — in the sacrament. This means that faith is both a prerequisite for our reception of the sacramental gifts and something God graciously bestows upon us through the sacrament. Logically this may sound a bit awkward, but it makes perfect sense theologically.

The celebration of the sacraments plays a key role in our Christian life as a whole. Many have experienced, though, that these acts have a special potential when we struggle with doubt and tribulation. In such situations, it will often make less sense to devote ourselves to meditations on abstract religious ideas. For most of us, there is a limit to how much lofty spirituality we can sustain when life gets hard. We may, however, be able to cling to the promise of the water of baptism. We may also be able to eat and drink what is offered us in the Eucharist — in times of crisis, solid nourishment is just as important in our spiritual as in our human life. And we can always *gaze* at the sacrament when bread and wine are elevated — assuming that seeing can be praying, too. At any rate, Eucharistic elevation is directed towards empirical sensation. And this actualizes an essential element in a materialist spirituality.

In this respect, I have to admit that it astonishes me that the sacraments in several versions of pastoral therapy have a quite marginal or perhaps even nonexistent role; relatively shallow psychological techniques often seem to be preferred. Now, there is certainly nothing wrong with psychology. On the contrary, all who are involved in pastoral care should listen carefully to qualified psychologists. But this should not lead to our ignoring the potential in the visualization and concretization of grace that takes place through the sacraments. Here I would especially like to refer to the consolation that people struggling with depression and guilt feelings can find in the sacrament of confession or reconciliation. While offering much-needed crisis aid to broken souls, the sacraments also have the capacity to reshape and reinvigorate our lives.

Philip Melanchthon, Martin Luther's main collaborator, describes ordination as a sacrament in the *Apology* of the Augsburg Confession. Yet, Lutherans normally settle with two or three sacraments — baptism, the Eucharist, and eventually confession. Within the Roman Catholic Church, seven sacraments are celebrated — i.e., baptism, the Eucharist, penance or reconciliation, confirmation, marriage, ordination, and the anointing of the sick. Seen from a Catholic viewpoint, all these practices are anchored in the work of the historic Jesus — if not always in a clearly defined act of institution. The difference in number is partly due to the fact that Lutherans tend to apply a more constricted sacramental concept. However, this may also be another example of the tension between breadth and focus within the universe of faith. Still, Catholics agree that baptism and the Eucharist are the chief sacraments.

At the same time, Catholic theology is careful to underscore that our Christian life as a whole has a sacramental foundation. Baptism provides access to the church as the sphere of grace, and needs no repetition. The Eucharist enables us to partake in the fruits of Christ's sacrifice; it should therefore be celebrated as often as possible — if normally not more than once a day. Confession grants us forgiveness of our sins and helps us to live a true Christian life. In confirmation, our baptismal pact is renewed. Marriage confers blessing on a crucial human relationship. Ordination contributes to the establishment of functioning and beneficial leadership. While there are several ordered services in the church, ordination in a more specific sense is applied only to the so-called threefold ministry of bishop, priest, and deacon. Finally, the anointing of the sick connects us with the healing power of God. This shows that the sacraments emerge as a red thread in our Christian existence, something that embraces us from birth to death. It also affirms that sacramental grace is available to us in all aspects and phases of life.

In the wake of this, Catholics insist that the church has a sacramental nature, too. As expressed by Henri de Lubac, Christ is God's sacrament and the church is "Christ's sacrament to us" — meaning that it is the space for his concrete presence among us and an indispensable instrument in the mediation of redemption. This does not imply that the church is attributed with divine status; it remains a means in the saving act of Christ. It does, however, play a key role in our Christian life — being the mother of faith and the place of salvation. When the church is understood as sacrament, the intention is primarily to emphasize its close relationship to Christ as his body on earth. Furthermore, theologians like Karl Rahner have been keen to describe the church as *sacramentum mundi* — a sacrament in and for the world. This approach suggests that the church's mission and service in and for the world belong integrally to its sacramental nature. Along such lines, the dynamic character of sacramentality is demonstrated.

Baptism is the *prima porta ecclesiae*, our once-and-for-all gate to the church and to grace. It can thus be described as a foundational sacrament — functioning as an initial presupposition of other bestowals of grace. Here our life in Christ begins through the mediation of the Holy Spirit. Even if there is a wide variety of spiritual gifts, there is no other "baptism in the Spirit" than the one that takes place with plain water. Subsequent to this, baptism makes us children of God. This happens like a birth, without any cooperation from our side. In and through baptism, God creates faith in us — once more in analogy with a *creatio ex nihilo*, as he created the world from nothing else than his love. Accordingly, the practice of baptizing children conveys an appropriate picture of what baptism is all about. This sacrament also implies that we are concretely united with Christ's death and resurrection: "We were buried therefore with him by baptism into death, so that as Christ was raised from the dead by the glory of the Father, we too might walk in newness of life" (Rom. 6:4). This is symbolized through our immersion in the water of baptism and our reappearance from this water. In addition to Romans 6, this view of baptism is reflected in Titus 3:4-7:

> . . . when the goodness and loving kindness of God our Savior appeared, he saved us, not because of deeds done by us in righteousness, but in virtue of his own mercy, by the washing of regeneration and renewal in the Holy Spirit, which he poured out upon us richly through Jesus Christ our Savior, so that we might be justified by his grace and become heirs in hope of eternal life.

I have already mentioned that baptism neither shall be nor needs to be repeated. However, this does not mean that the sacrament of baptism is reduced to a past event or a previous stage. Quite on the contrary, our continued life in Christ can only be lived on the basis of baptism. This is the solid and never failing foundation of our Christian existence. Accordingly, conversion can be seen as a return to baptismal grace. Yet, this return is neither static nor solely retrospective. It implies continual struggle against sin as well as spiritual growth. In this way, we are enabled to share in the "newness of life." Here we are provided with yet another example of the transforming nature of sacramental grace. Such grace is also a power that works holiness and renewal in us.

This directs us towards another crucial sacramental act, namely confession or the sacrament of reconciliation. Regrettably, there is much evidence that this sacrament has become somewhat marginalized. Formerly, a habitual phrase in American movies went approximately like this: "Bless me, Father, for I have sinned — it's been twenty days since my last confession." Today, a more accurate expression would perhaps be: "Bless me, Father, for I have sinned — it's been twenty *years* since my last confession." At any rate, we need to rekindle the awareness of the significant role of this sacrament.

What, then, does confession have to offer when we are allowed to believe that God has already pardoned us in Christ? First, it mediates forgiveness through the priest's words in a far more palpable way than abstract ideas ever can do. Thus seen, confession is not a heavy duty, but rather an event of joy and freedom. Second, confession or penance forms a vital part of our struggle against sin and its power. This is symbolized by the penitential punishments that the priest can confer on us. The point here is not a vain attempt to "deserve" salvation, but to visualize our efforts to be freed from sin. This is a vital part of the growth that should accompany our Christian life. Third, the sacrament of reconciliation is an assurance that we are reconciled with the Father in the Son through the Spirit: "If we confess our sins, he is faithful and just, and will forgive our sins and cleanse us from all unrighteousness" (1 John 1:9). The laying on of hands serves as an expression of the Father's boundless love for his children. And through this wondrous act, there is a direct path to reconciliation with our fellow human beings and the whole of creation. This is affirmed in the account of the message and service of reconciliation in 2 Corinthians 5:11-21.

Along these lines, confession is capable of conveying a crucial sense that faith really has to do with life. This applies to our personal lives as well as those of our neighbors and the world. It further affirms that God is not only concerned with us when we behave decently. As a matter of fact, he may be closer to us in the darkest moments of our existence. And as the Catholic authors Graham Greene and Shusaku Endo insist: Anyone can love the nice and pleasant, but it takes a God to love the despicable and thoroughly revolting.

As fragile creatures, our human life is always threatened and ultimately it will expire. However, both when we are struggling with more or less serious illness and when our life fades, the anointing of the sick — formerly the last rites — provides us with solid comfort. Surely, this sacrament is no guarantee that we will be healed. But it reminds us of and connects us with the healing power of God, he who always knows what is best for his children. And it reflects the reality that Christ remains at our side, especially in our most miserable moments. Moreover, the anointing suggests that the physical death of those who are in Christ is not the end; it is rather a transition or even a new beginning. For our spiritual life continues, in the shape of a redeemed body — setting us free to worship in spirit and truth. On this basis, Paul exclaims: "'Death is swallowed up in victory.' 'O death, where is thy victory? O death, where is thy sting?' The sting of death is sin, and the power of sin is the law. But thanks be to God, who gives us the victory through our Lord Jesus Christ" (1 Cor. 15:54b-57).

Much could be said about the remaining sacramental acts. And I shall soon take a closer look at the Eucharist. Otherwise, however, this will have to suffice here. My key aim is to demonstrate the essential role of sacramentality in general and the individual sacraments in particular within our Christian life. This is especially important in view of a materialist spirituality. As already indicated, the sacraments constitute the concrete stuff or *materia* of such spirituality. A better corrective over against falsely spiritualized attitudes can hardly be conceived. And once more, the incarnation forms the basis: Jesus Christ became a human being like us, and still comes to us through outward and visible means and through signs taken from the created earth. The Jesus who meets us in the sacraments is "full of grace and truth" (John 1:14). This interaction is vital. For while grace without truth — the truth about our lives — may degenerate to sentimentality, truth without grace may end up as rigid moralism.

All the sacramental acts belong to a whole Christian life. It therefore makes no sense to rank them. Still, the Eucharist has a key standing — not least within the framework of a materialist spirituality. This mainly depends on the Eucharist's being the sacrament of the church in a special sense. It makes and recreates the church; it is the primary ecclesial icon. The church is never more church than when it celebrates the Lord's Supper, being the peak of ecclesiality. For we become the body of Christ on earth when we eat his body and drink his blood. The Eucharist also has a special importance in our spiritual life. Practically speaking, this is due to the fact that it is the most frequently celebrated sacrament — at least for Catholics of varying observances. More importantly, however, here the threads of our life in Christ are gathered; here we receive the food we so desperately need on our journey to heaven; and here we have communion with him who is the cornerstone and the solid foundation of our faith. Through this communion, we also have fellowship with each other. As already indicated, this sacramental mystery is realized when we share in his body and blood — the blood that is shed for the sake of world.

Christ is the definite core and the central content of the Lord's Supper. He is the one who invites all to come; he prepares the meal;

and he is himself the food in which we partake at the table. In the Eucharist, Jesus is present as the incarnated Son of God — i.e., as perfect God, our Lord, and perfect human being, our brother. His presence in the sacrament cannot be reduced to the level of spiritualized feelings or abstract ideas. Like all forms of meal- or table-fellowship, the Lord's Supper implies a close and concrete communion between persons. And once more, Christ's presence is attached to a regular feature in the life of many people — namely the act of sharing a meal and eating together.

From this fellowship there is a direct path to our obligation to share our bread with those who lack what they need for their daily existence. As members of the body of Christ, he who is the bread of life, we are obliged to share our bread with others. This is a question of ethics and morals, but it is also an integral and indispensable part of Eucharistic theology. As we have seen, this is affirmed in Paul's teaching on the Eucharist in 1 Corinthians 11. In a world where a small minority are wildly rich and a huge and growing majority struggle with desperate poverty, this commitment becomes particularly vital.

At the core of all this is Christ's concrete presence. Already the disciples on their way to Emmaus just after the death of Jesus experienced this. At first, they did not realize that it was the risen Lord who walked together with them. But when he took the bread and broke it — just as we do in our celebration of the Eucharist, their eyes were opened and they recognized him (cf. Luke 24:13-35). Something very similar happens when we break the bread in the Lord's Supper. Then we too recognize Jesus, because he in this meal is closer to us than ever. And this depends on the fact that "the bread which we break . . . [is] a participation in the body of Christ" (1 Cor. 10:16).

Christ's presence in the Eucharist does not only apply to the meal event in a more general sense — and it cannot be reduced to the level of mere symbolism. This presence is chiefly connected to and expressed through the elements, namely bread and wine or what we eat and drink. This is the gist of the doctrine of the real presence. In my view, the question of *when* the transformation of bread and wine into the body and blood of Christ takes place is of less importance; the key concern is *that* this happens within the context of our celebration. Here we are confronted with a sacramental mystery that Christians have tried to explain in varying ways. These explanations only become divisive when they come across as the opposite — i.e., not as explanations, but as concealments or even denials of the real presence.

Simultaneously, it must be underlined that we cannot be too specific in regard to the real presence and its implications. In his moving novel *The Power and the Glory* (1940), Graham Greene describes a shabby "whiskey priest" who serves among poor and oppressed people in southern Mexico. The only thing that has retained a certain meaning in the ministry of this sad figure is his commission to "(put) God in the mouths of men." Some may find this expression a bit over the top. As far as I can gather, however, it is an appropriate way of describing the Eucharist and the real presence. In a partly similar manner, the saying that we become what we eat can be applied to the Eucharist.

As already indicated, the concrete presence of Christ in the elements of the Eucharist is the reason why our prayer *Agnus Dei* (Lamb of God) is directed also to Christ at the altar — he who is so close that he can be eaten and drunk. And when bread and wine are elevated by the priest, it is Christ who is lifted — in order that we shall see him and respond in prayer and by lifting our hearts. Admittedly, the Eucharist is first and foremost a meal, and the elements are food to be consumed. But it should not be ruled out that the things that carry the presence of Christ can also serve in a fruitful way as focal points for our prayer, devotion, and meditation. This presupposes that we do not worship the sacrament as such, but rather Christ in his presence in the sacrament. According to Catholic theology, this presence continues from the moment of consecration until the elements are consumed. This is the reason why the bread is kept in a Tabernacle.

The Gospel of John can be seen as brimming with sacramental theology. Christ is both "living water" and "the bread of life." While the first of these expressions may allude to baptism, the second one is presumably anchored in and aims at the Eucharist. I quote the key passage John 6:52-58:

> The Jews then disputed among themselves, saying, "How can this man give us his flesh to eat?" So Jesus said to them, "Truly, truly, I say to you, unless you eat the flesh of the Son of man and drink his blood, you have no life in you; he who eats my flesh and drinks my blood has eternal life, and I will raise him up at the last day. For my flesh is food indeed, and my blood is drink indeed. He who eats my

flesh and drinks my blood abides in me, and I in him. As the living
Father sent me, and I live because of the Father, so he who eats me
will live because of me. This is the bread which came down from
heaven, not such as the fathers ate and died; he who eats this bread
will live for ever."

When the real presence is so central, it must be concretely and visibly
manifested in the way we celebrate the Eucharist. Admittedly, worse
things have happened to the body of Christ than being dropped on the
floor. Yet, our handling of the elements is our way of showing that we
are serious about the real presence. For Martin Luther, this was an essential concern. What happened to chaplain Hans Besserer in his first
presiding at the Lord's Supper in Eisleben is an affirmation of this. The
young chaplain was probably both nervous and a bit clumsy, so he lost
an oblate at the floor. And since people at that time first went to confession, an exact number had been consecrated. In confusion, I believe,
Besserer replaced the lost oblate by an unconsecrated one. After the
service, however, he found the piece of bread. And not quite knowing
what to do with it, he placed it in the box where the unconsecrated wa-
fers were kept. When Luther heard about this, the chaplain was immediately excommunicated because of "Zwinglian heresies." This suggests
that a dominant practice among Lutheran clergy in Norway and probably also other places — namely putting consecrated oblates back with
the unconsecrated ones — was a reason for excommunication.

Admittedly, Luther rejected sacramental devotion. But he accepted
elevation of bread and wine. Moreover, the stressing of the *in usu* principle
— in use — does not mean that the sacramental presence is limited to the
meal, but that the elements should be used in accordance with their intention — namely as food. Still, bread was kept for the communion of the
sick. And most importantly, the Reformer saw the biblical words of institution as words of consecration — and not as a somewhat inferior way of
preaching the gospel to slow or dense people who were not quite capable
of grasping the message. In general, there is much evidence suggesting that
Luther remained strongly committed to a Catholic Eucharistic practice
throughout his life. At any rate, he stated that he would much rather
"drink blood with the Pope than wine with the enthusiasts." This does not
always seem to be the case in contemporary Lutheranism.

In terms of Eucharistic practice, it should be noted that the Roman Catholic Church in many cases continues to give only the bread to the faithful in the Mass. This is basically a practical thing — aiming at a proper handling of the elements that carry the presence of Christ. I could think of some Lutheran congregations that might have something to learn from this. Here it is further assumed that those who eat Christ's body in the consecrated bread share in his blood, too. Still, it must be emphasized that the whole and full meaning of the sacrament would be better expressed if both bread and wine were distributed to all. At this point, Catholics can learn from the Lutheran practice.

Many people struggle to believe that a tiny piece of bread — normally in the rather dreary shape of an oblate — and a mouthful of wine can accommodate the mystery of salvation in its fullness. This entices them to engage in a restless hunt for more tremulous spiritual experiences. But the oblate is capable of delivering what it pledges. Here Christ is really and truly present; here the big wondrous act occurs; here we share in the gifts of salvation. I cannot imagine any other event where grace is as accessible as in the Eucharist. At first glance, the whole thing can appear as painfully modest and inconspicuous. But looking more closely, many will realize — and have realized — that having Christ "put in our mouths" speaks more strongly and more clearly than even the most ferocious ecstatic feelings. This particularly applies to those among us who are heavily burdened. For if we cannot believe, we can at least swallow . . .

I have maintained that the doctrine of the real presence is at the core of the Lord's Supper. At the same time, this key sacrament includes an abundance of motives. Our focus on the real presence must, therefore, never take place at the expense of the vast richness of the Eucharist. An exaggerated preoccupation with the forgiveness of sins is yet another example of a somewhat impoverished Eucharistic theology. Although this is a crucial concern, it is not the whole story. Here there is a need for open comprehensiveness rather than single-mindedness.

One of the most fundamental aspects of the Eucharist is that it relates to and connects us with Christ's sacrifice. On the one hand, this sacrifice neither can be nor needs to be repeated. At Calvary, Christ laid the foundation for our redemption once and for all. On the other hand, the offering at the cross cannot be reduced to a distant and isolated point in history. It must also somehow be present among us today, so that we can share in its fruits. And this is exactly what happens in the

Eucharist. This does not signify that the unique Calvary event is repeated or reiterated. What is at stake here is a *sacramental representation* of the one sacrifice of Christ. His offering can only be at the center of the Eucharist if it is made effectively present in our celebration. Furthermore, the remembrance *(anamnesis)* that is referred to in Jesus' words of institution — "Do this in my remembrance" (Luke 22:19) — is not only a question of keeping a past event in our memory or our mind as a largely abstract idea. This is a living and concrete remembrance, denoting that it includes the present-making or the sacramental representation of Christ's great sacrifice for the life of the world. Also in this sense, the institution words transcend the level of preaching.

Additionally, the Eucharist is the sacrament of thanksgiving *(eucharistia)* in which we offer our thanks to the Father for the great things he has done for us in Christ. This is our response to the Paschal sacrifice. Hence, our Eucharistic celebration should be filled with joy and happiness — counteracting the omnipresence of sin. Furthermore, the Holy Spirit plays a vital role in the Eucharist. This is expressed in its so-called *epicletic* dimension, which mainly pertains to our prayer to God that he shall shed his life-giving Spirit over the sacramental gifts. Here we face yet another affirmation that the Spirit works through outward means. Moreover, we have already stressed that the Eucharist is the sacrament of fellowship; it is a celebration of the church as Christ's body. In this connection, we enjoy communion with and participation in the Triune God. And this participation points towards our human community — obliging us to seek fellowship with each other, all human beings, and the whole of creation. In the wake of this, the earthliness of the sacramental elements shows that the world is present in our celebration. Lastly, the Eucharist is the foretaste of the heavenly feast — reflecting its eschatological character. Along these lines, we get a glimpse of the immense richness of our Eucharistic celebration.

I have previously stated that sacramental grace is transforming grace. In the Eucharist, a threefold transformation takes place: First, plain bread and wine become the flesh and blood of Christ. This applies to the inner substance of the elements and not their outer form — thus, implicitly witnessing to the transformation of the whole of creation back to its original integrity. Second, a far-from-perfect church becomes Christ's body. As we have seen, this crucial ecclesial event is meant in a very concrete sense. And third, the transformation of our broken lives and our fragile bodies into the full life and the redeemed bodies that God has in mind for us is initiated. This last transformation will not be completed until Christ returns in order to fulfill his work. But the Eucharist provides us with an assurance that this is no pie in the sky; it is rather firm sacramental reality.

We have now seen that Christ is fully and really present in the Eucharist through elementary and empirically perceptible things like bread and wine. The Eucharist is furthermore the sacrament of the church; it is our main ecclesial icon, which makes and recreates the church. And it directs us towards our responsibility for our fellow human beings and the whole of creation — not only as an ensuing consequence, but also as an integral part of our Eucharistic celebration and theology. Here there are no traces of falsely spiritualized concepts or vague abstraction; this is an indispensable example of *corporeal* and *embodied* faith. Accordingly, a better expression of a materialist spirituality can hardly be found. Such spirituality therefore emerges as a eucharistically anchored piety — forming an essential part of its sacramental foundation.

This brings us back to sacramentality and the other sacraments. On the one hand, the Eucharist can be seen as the key sacrament in our Christian life. On the other hand, it is clearly related to other sacramental acts. This primarily applies to baptism: Only those who have become members of Christ's body in baptism can participate in the manifestation and celebration of this body in the Eucharist. At the same time, our commitment to child baptism is a strong argument in favor of including children here. Thus, the age of first communion should in my opinion be significantly lowered. Moreover, there is a close interaction between the Eucharist and the sacrament of reconciliation, calling for more frequent use of confession. And ordination provides us with the ordained ministry — or ministries — which is a prerequisite for our Eucharistic celebration.

At the core of a materialist spirituality is the basic corporeality of the sacraments and their elements. Here it must be reiterated that this corporeality cannot be seen as a somewhat inferior form of the paramount task of preaching the gospel, let alone as a help to those of us who may be a bit slow or dense — at the level of the *Biblia pauperum*, the use of images to communicate the message of the Bible to those who could not read. Quite on the contrary, the palpable nature of the elements contributes essentially to our understanding of grace — or, more precisely, to its common accessibility. And even if God's promise in Christ constitutes all sacraments, the sacramental acts cannot be interpreted as mere repetitions of our gospel preaching. At this point, we are rather talking about a fruitful dialectic that is grounded in the abundance of faith.

Finally, the sacraments are not narrowly "religious" entities; they are related to human life and the world. Through earthly elements we are reminded of the vital path from creation to the creator and then back again to creation. In opening up for an encounter with God, there is a sacramentality to creation. Moreover, especially marriage witnesses to the sacramental potential of human relations. And confession shows that there is a close connection between our reconciliation with God in Christ and the desperate need for reconciliation in our present world. This reflects the fact that our lives — in light of the transforming renewal that takes place in and through the sacraments — also carry a sacramental promise. In this way, sacramentality and mission are linked.

Literature

Auer, Johann, and Joseph Ratzinger. *Allgemeine Sakramentenlehre und das Mysterium der Eucharistie.* Kleine Katholische Dogmatik, Bd. VI. Regensburg: Friedrich Pustet, 1971.

Boff, Leonardo. *Sacraments of Life — Life of the Sacraments.* Portland, OR: Pastoral Press, 1987.

Coffrey, David. *The Sacrament of Reconciliation.* Collegeville, MN: Liturgical Press, 2001.

Diestelmann, Jürgen. *Actio Sacramentalis: Die Verwaltung des Heiligen Abendmahles nach den Prinzipien Martin Luthers in der Zeit bis zur Konkordienformel.* Gross Oessingen: Verlag des lutherischen Buchhandlung H. Harms, 1996.

Irwin, Kevin. *Models of the Eucharist.* Mahwah, NJ: Paulist Press, 2005.

John Paul II. *Ecclesia de Eucharistia: On the Eucharist in Its Relationship to the Church* (Encyclical). Boston: Pauline Books, 2003.

Power, David N. *Sacrament: The Language of God's Giving.* New York: Crossroad, 1999.

Rahner, Karl. *The Church and the Sacraments.* London: Continuum, 1974.

Schlink, Edmund. *Die Lehre von der Taufe.* Kassel: Johannes Stauda-Verlag, 1969.

Schillebeeckx, Edward. *The Eucharist.* London: Continuum, 2005.

8 Prayer as Language and Liturgy as Song

On the Meaning of Worship

Common and public liturgical worship is absolutely essential to the whole people of God as well as to individual Christians. In my own feeble attempts to maintain a minimum of personal piety, the collective nature of the liturgy has for a long time played a key role. Here I have found a fertile environment for what I was unable to produce on my own. Today, however, traditional liturgies are by many considered to be hopelessly outdated in regard to our daily lives and the contemporary world. There is, therefore, a strong urge for renewal in most churches. Now, parts of our liturgies can be somewhat obsolete, but this is not always the case. Actually, the recurring complaints in this field may rather indicate an increasing lack of liturgical consciousness. Further, a measure of continuity is doubtless required in this field. And even if one-sidedly retrospective attitudes are a dead-end, hectic and shallow modernization is not the only conceivable path to a meaningful worship life.

Yet, I seriously doubt that the recent reintroduction of the Tridentine Mass is a good thing. Surely, it would not do any harm if this version were celebrated occasionally — it could even be enriching. The problem, however, is that it might entice further growth in Catholic nostalgicism. Personally, I clearly prefer the post–Vatican II Missal of Pope Paul VI — not least since it reflects the vital theological outcome of the Council. At the same time, I would like to underline that the present praise-song regime in many Christian groups can appear as more bothering than the rekindling of pre-conciliar practices. In this connection, mantras with ten words and fewer than ten notes are forced upon us — even though they desperately lack spiritual depth or cultural sustainability. Once more I am tempted to exclaim: God be praised for boredom!

My proposal here would rather be along the lines of continuity in content and renewal in form. This implies that the authentic ideals of liturgical worship are still valid, especially in view of the liturgy's basic structure. At the same time, I welcome contributions from contemporary or modernist culture in regard to the form of the liturgy. This would help us to include the world — God's world — in our worship life and our celebration of the Mass in a palpable way. Without such inclusion, we simply cannot worship in spirit and truth. Moreover, art is capable of assisting us in identifying a constructive intermediate approach between a deficient sense of history and pure nostalgia. Let me add that church services must reflect a deep sense of and esteem for holiness, excluding profanation. But I am inclined to believe that holiness can be quite a bit more robust than we often assume. Respect for the holy is not the same as barren cautiousness or sterile anxiety.

In the following, I aim at exploring the central intention of the liturgy, the sign language of the church, and the liturgy's relevance as an act of prayer. Here I will base myself on a crucial Catholic concern: Nothing that takes place in the Mass and our worship life as a whole is random or arbitrary. On the contrary, even the most ordinary acts or signs carry deep spiritual meaning. Such signs cannot be considered as hefty "effects," and their meaning does not have to be dug out through soaring spiritualized interpretation. Liturgical signs are open to plain and elementary empirical perception. In the Mass, what we see and hear, taste and smell is of crucial significance. Additionally, this language is — at least formally speaking — similar to human languages. In the wake of this, I would like to repeat that God within the framework of our worship first and foremost deals with us as a collective, a people or a body, and not as secluded individuals. Therefore, our personal taste — what we immediately "like" — is not the sole criterion in judging what is a good and appropriate way of worshiping.

Already these introductory deliberations affirm that a materialist spirituality must be seen as a liturgically anchored piety. In the previous chapter, we noted that this applies fully to the sacraments or the means of grace. The liturgy, however, with its fundamental structure and concrete outward signs, provides the required framework for our sacramental celebration. And all parts of the liturgy point towards and emphasize the Eucharist, which is its core and peak. Accordingly, sacramentality and liturgical awareness presuppose each other mutually within the context of a materialist spirituality.

The liturgy can be described as the church's song — at least when it is being sung and not only spoken. And song adds life; it *is* life. In this connection, the melody with its score is not only a practical framework and a more or less beautiful formality. Here we can learn from the modernist idea of "absolute music" (Carl Dahlhaus) — or the insistence that music cannot be reduced to the level of harmonic accompaniment to words. At the core of church music, there is a close interaction or partnership between words and tunes. Especially in the liturgy, it becomes clear that the outward form carries deep spiritual meaning. Here I am again reminded of St. Benedict's crucial insight that the purpose of the liturgy is that our minds shall be made to conform to our voices — not the other way round. Further, St. Augustine claims that those who sing, primarily in the liturgy, pray twice as strongly — *qui cantat bis orat*. This confirms both the power of singing together and what many of us have experienced when we are really lifted by the liturgy. At a concert at Castel Gandolfo in the early fall of 2007, Pope Benedict XVI made a partly similar, if more general observation: "Music has the power to lead us back . . . to the Creator of all harmony, creating a resonance within us which is like being in tune with the beauty and truth of God."

The liturgy reflects the transforming capacity that chiefly is attached to our celebration of the Eucharist: First, by singing together, individuals are transformed into one body — namely the body of Christ. This is the reason why Paul describes the church and the careful interaction between its members by the image of a symphony orchestra: "If even lifeless instruments, such as the flute or the harp, do not give distinct notes, how will any one know what is played?" (1 Cor. 14:7). Second, through liturgical chant, our minds are cleansed and made open to God. Here it should be added, though, that this does not only apply to Gregorian melodies, but clearly also to good contemporary liturgies and modernist church music. Despite invaluable treasures from the past, one-sided retrospective nostalgicism is a dead-end for a church that is called to serve the world in its present shape. Third, just as with the Eucharist, the liturgy witnesses to and celebrates the grand ultimate transformation of the whole creation that will take place when Christ returns in order to fulfill his work.

What, then, is the liturgy of the church all about in a more specific theological sense? This cannot be expressed through a singular formula or an exact definition; a vast richness of components and motives is at stake here. Yet, some concerns of basic importance must be emphasized at this point.

First, the foundation and the core of the liturgy is the most precious gift and the most beautiful thing that can be envisioned, namely the Father's offering of his only Son for the life of the world — or the story of the one who gives his life for the many. This determines the whole structure and logic of our worship — from the initial rites, via the liturgy of the word and the credo, to the liturgy of the Eucharist or the offertory. But it is particularly connected with and expressed through the sacramental representation of Christ's sacrifice that takes place in our Eucharistic celebration. As already suggested, this is the main reason why services without the Lord's Supper may seem somewhat truncated.

Our participation in the sacrifice of Christ is a pure gift; it is something that God gives to us freely and that we receive in and through faith. At the same time, gifts are normally supposed to generate a reaction on the side of the receiver in the form of appreciation and gratitude. This is also the case in the offering at the cross, the greatest gift that can be conceived. We respond to God's ultimate gift in Christ through our offering of praise and thanksgiving. Surely, these offerings are not on the same level. Yet, they belong together within a dialectical relationship. This interaction between God's gift and our gratitude, between *sacrificium* and *sacramentum*, is essential to the dynamics of the liturgy. It is also a vital part of our "spiritual worship": "I appeal to you . . . brethren, by the mercies of God, to present your bodies as a living sacrifice, holy and acceptable to God, which is your spiritual worship" (Rom. 12:1).

In this connection, the priest operates on Christ's behalf — *in persona Christi*. His acts, therefore, reflect God's merciful deeds towards us. This also applies to many of the things that fill the space of the church. Generally, what we do in the Mass represents our reply to the work of the Triune God. Surely, God's saving activity is beyond comparison most important here. Yet, we — the people — are not only passive recipients, let alone marionettes. Many consider church worship as some kind of spiritual gas station where we swing in every Sunday morning in order to be "filled up." Over against such ideas, it must be underlined that we are not laid-back consumers in the liturgy. We are active subjects or participants in the sense that we respond to God's grace through plain liturgical acts and affirmations. This is an integral part of our communion with the Father through the Son in the Spirit.

Second, the liturgy provides the necessary framework for our celebration of the means of grace. As pointed out in the previous chapter, these means in general and the Eucharist in particular constitute and so to speak make or create the church. But they are normally only available within the context of liturgical worship. Accordingly, it can be argued that the church — at least in practice — is constituted by its worship life and the liturgy of the Mass. Within the liturgy, the word calls us to communion with God and reveals his good will to us. Through baptism we become members of the body of Christ. Confession — also in its collective form — implies a call to holiness and to live a true Christian life. And in the celebration of the paramount sacrament of the Eucharist, we benefit from the fruits of Christ's sacrifice through the plain acts of eating and drinking. Thus seen, sacramentality and liturgy emerge as clearly interconnected entities.

Third, the liturgy aims at incorporating and expressing the drama of salvation in its fullness, nothing less. This occurs when we actively remember, recapitulate, and celebrate God's gracious deeds on our behalf. Worship is, therefore, not a snug Christian "show." It reflects the greatest drama of being and becomes itself a part of this drama — not in the sense of repetition, but in the form of a dynamic sacramental and liturgical representation. The retelling of the key events of salvation takes place in each worship service, but also within a wider framework. The classical daily prayer of the church — the office of the hours, from early morning to late night — plays a key role at this point. Earlier, we could often trust that our parents prayed for us. But this responsibility primarily rests with mother church, granting us assurance and comfort. The liturgical year is another vital factor here. This year is essential to the rhythm and completeness of faith. Hence, its current dismantling into an endless series of hardly distinguishable "theme services" must be regretted. This is just as meaningless as cutting an act from a play by Henrik Ibsen.

When the drama of salvation is recreated, the central content of our faith is actualized. This content is not only defined through doctrinal statements, with the more or less constructive assistance of dogmatic theology. Here too the church's liturgy plays a crucial role. This is especially attached to our reciting of the creed, together and with one voice. But it also applies to the liturgy and its structure as a whole. In this manner, the old saying that the law of prayer is the law of faith — *lex orandi, lex credendi* — is confirmed. Or — in the words of Prosper of Aquitaine (fifth century): The law of prayer determines the law of belief, stressing the theological importance of liturgy even more strongly. On a similar note, St. Irenaeus maintains that Christian doctrine conforms to the Eucharist, while the Eucharist in turn confirms the church's doctrine.

Fourth, in the wake of this we are directed towards what is labeled as liturgical theology. During the last decades, this approach has become increasingly central in a wide ecumenical perspective — being associated with names like Alexander Schmemann, Aidan Kavanagh, Geoffrey Wainwright, Gordon Lathrop, and David Fagerberg. In his important book *What Is Liturgical Theology? A Study in Methodology*, Fagerberg stresses that what is at stake here is not "a theology *of* worship," but "a theology *from* worship." The main object of this approach is not liturgically anchored worship in a narrow sense, but rather God, humanity, and the world. Moreover, the fundamental theological relevance of the liturgy is due to its being the context in which God's revelation is continually manifested.

Aidan Kavanagh contributes further to an elucidation of liturgical theology — and thus also to a definition of liturgy and liturgical acts as such:

> . . . what emerges most directly from an assembly's liturgical act is not a new species of theology among others. It is *theologia* itself. Nor is it inchoate and raw, despite the fact that it is always open to endless further specification and exploitation by human minds. This may be the reason why Alexander Schmemann wrote that the liturgy ". . . is not an 'authority' or a *locus theologicus;* it is the ontological condition of theology, of the proper understanding of *kerygma*, of the Word of God, because it is in the Church, of which the *leitourgia* is the expression and the life, that the sources of theology are functioning precisely as sources."

[. . .]

What results from a liturgical act is not only "meaning," but an ecclesial transaction with reality, a transaction whose ramifications escape over the horizon of the present, beyond the act itself, to overflow even the confines of the local assembly into universality. The act both changes and outstrips the assembly in which it occurs. The assembly adjusts to that change, becoming different from what it was before the act happened.

[. . .]

Thus is the faith kept as something always alive in the present. Thus is memory mediated ever new as tradition. Thus is conversion made a sustained quality in the assembly itself. Thus is divine purpose served in the real world of whatever epoch. Thus is the Gift always given and received. Thus do structures arise. Hence theology of the second order flows. (*On Liturgical Theology*, pp. 75-95)

Fifth, along these lines liturgical theology verifies that the church's liturgy contains a recapitulation and celebration of the drama of salvation. At the same time, it reminds us that the earth plays a key role in this drama. This compares to the basic theological fact that salvation cannot be limited to individual souls, but aims at the redemption of creation. It is also the reason why we cannot worship in spirit and truth unless God's world is truly present among us. This vital aspect is recalled in our prayers for the world; it is visualized through the sacramental elements which are taken from creation; and it is concretized when most liturgies conclude with sending us out into the world in order to serve.

Seen in this perspective, there is a close interconnection between *missa* — the Mass — and *missio* — our mission, or between liturgy and the diaconate. The latter is basically grounded in the liturgy and the Eucharist, while the liturgy aims at diaconal service. Accordingly, the just-mentioned sending at the end of the liturgy cannot be seen as a less important or secondary supplement. In establishing a vital link to our daily life and the world, it rather belongs to the logic of the liturgy. It further reminds us that our mission in the world is an integral and indispensable part of the church's existence. Within the space of the church, we participate in God's abundant gifts to us. We are, therefore, sent out to share our goods with our fellow human beings. All this is anchored in "the ministry of reconciliation" as described in 2 Corinthians 5:11-21.

In this way, the church is visualized as *sacramentum mundi* — a sacrament in and for the world.

The Catholic philosopher and theologian Romano Guardini contributed significantly in paving the way to the liturgical renewal that took place in the wake of Vatican II. Not least in regard to the practical meaning of the liturgy, Guardini is an excellent mentor. I quote from one of his main works:

> The primary and exclusive aim of the liturgy is not the expression of the individual's reverence and worship for God. [. . .] It does not even rest with the collective groups, composed of numerous individuals, who periodically achieve a limited and intermittent unity in their capacity as the congregation of a church. The liturgical entity consists rather of the united body of the faithful as such — the Church — a body which infinitely outnumbers the mere congregation. [. . .] In the liturgy God is to be honored by the body of the faithful, and the latter is in its turn to derive sanctification from this act of worship. It is important that this objective nature of the liturgy should be fully understood. (*The Spirit of the Liturgy*, p. 19)

Guardini's strong affirmation of the collective nature of the liturgy corresponds with my previous observation that God within the context of church worship primarily deals with us as a body and not as individuals, not even as the sum of individuals. This does not mean that personal taste and needs are excluded, but signifies that such angles must be subordinated to the concerns of the fellowship as a whole. And it points towards "the objective nature" of the liturgy.

Furthermore, Guardini identifies other vital concerns: The liturgy teaches us that "the prayer of a corporate body must be sustained by thought" — alluding to the principle that the law of prayer is the law of faith. He adds: "Only thought is universally current and consistent, and . . . remains suited, to a degree, to every intelligence. If prayer in common, therefore, is to prove beneficial to the majority, it must be primarily directed by thought, and not by feeling" (pp. 21-22). Furthermore, "prayer is beneficial only when it rests on the bedrock of truth. This is not meant in a purely negative sense that it must be free from error; in addition to this, it must spring from the fullness of truth." "Here, too, the liturgy is our teacher. It condenses into prayer the entire body of religious truth. Indeed, it is nothing else but truth expressed in terms of prayer" — referring to the liturgy's comprehensive Trinitarian foundation (pp. 22-24). And finally, even if "[the emphasizing of] the necessity of thought . . . must not be allowed to degenerate into the mere frigid domination of reason," ". . . liturgical emotion is . . . exceedingly instructive. It has its moments of supreme climax. . . . But as a rule it is controlled and subdued" (p. 25). Both the collective nature and the sober character of the liturgy appeal to a materialist spirituality.

In the final paragraph of the book, the following view is set forth:

> The liturgy has something in itself reminiscent of the stars, of their eternally fixed and even course, of their inflexible order, of their profound silence, and of the infinite space in which they are poised. It is only in appearance, however, that the liturgy is so detached and untroubled by the actions and strivings and moral position of men. For in reality it knows that those who live by it will be true and spiritually sound, and at peace to the depths of their being; and that when they leave its sacred confines to enter life they will be men of courage. (*The Spirit of the Liturgy*, p. 95)

This actualizes the essential moral implications or fruits of the liturgy. Through the transformation of our lives that is inaugurated here, we are both committed and equipped to serve our fellow human beings and creation as a whole.

Finally, Paul reminds us that "we walk by faith, not by sight" (2 Cor. 5:7). This explains the present ambiguity of faith. And until Christ returns in order to fulfill his work, all attempts to escape from this ambiguity are doomed to fail. Still, I have already suggested that the ambiguous nature of our Christian existence is transcended at one point — e.g., in our sacramental celebration within the framework of liturgical worship. This does not mean that the ambiguity of our faith life is removed altogether. But it implies that we are enabled to see things — if indirectly, as in a mirror. Moreover, we are granted the ability to sense spiritual stuff through empirical perception. This is what happened to the disciples who met the risen Christ on their way to Emmaus; they recognized him when he broke the bread (cf. Luke 24:13-35). A similar thing takes place within the liturgy of the Mass —

thus, being our Emmaus-experience. This is of special importance to a materialist spirituality.

The rich sign language of the church is particularly connected with our liturgical worship as well as the church building and its equipment. It expresses both God's gracious deeds towards us and our response to these deeds. On the one hand, this language requires a certain measure of initial explanation — or, rather, people must be "reminded" of what these plain acts and symbols mean. On the other hand, I have already indicated that such efforts must not be allowed to lead to our sign language being exposed to false spiritualization. This language is also grounded in elementary empirical perception: in things we see and hear, taste and smell. It is, therefore, "democratic" and accessible to all. Furthermore, it is congruent with common human sign systems or basic acts: We wash when we have become unclean; we wish to eat when we are hungry; and we touch each other — as in the practice of the laying on of hands — as a symbol of affection and closeness. Soaring spiritualized interpretation will only contribute to the complication of our sign language. And then it loses its original intention.

In exploring this language and its implications further, I once more quote from a contribution of Romano Guardini — i.e., his book on "sacred signs":

> This little book . . . was written to help open up the world of the liturgy. That world will never be made accessible by accounts of how certain rites and prayers came into existence and under what influences, or by explanations of the ideas underlying liturgical practices. Those ideas may be true and profound, but they are not apparent in the present liturgy, and can be deduced from it only by scholarly research. The liturgy is not a matter of ideas, but of actual things, and of actual things as they now are, and not as they were in the past. It is a continuous movement carried on by and through us, and its forms and actions issue from our human nature. To show how it arose and developed brings us no nearer to it, and no more does this or that learned interpretation. What does help is to discern in the living liturgy what underlies the visible sign, to discover the soul from the body, the hidden and spiritual from the external and material. The liturgy has taken its outward

shape from a divine and hidden series of happenings. It is sacramental in its nature.

So the procedure that avails is to study those actions that are still in present day use, those visible signs which believers have received and made their own and use to express the "invisible grace." For this it is not liturgical scholarship that is needed, — though the two things are not separable, — but liturgical education. We need to be shown how, or by some means incited, to see and feel and make the sacred signs ourselves.

[. . .]

One person who could do [this] . . . both better and more appropriately, would be a mother who had herself been trained in the liturgy. She could teach her child the right way to make the sign of the cross, make him see what it is in himself the lighted candle stands for, show him in his little human person how to stand and carry himself in his Father's house, and never at any point with the least touch of aestheticism, simply as something the child sees, something he does, and not as an idea to hang gestures on.

. . . the approach to the liturgy is not by being told about it but by taking part in it.

To learn to see, to learn to do, these are the fundamental "skills" that make the groundwork for all the rest. The doing must of course be lightened by lucid instruction and rooted in Catholic tradition, which they learn from their courses in history. And "doing" does not mean "practicing" in order to get a thing right. Doing is basic; it includes the whole human person with all his creative powers. It is the outcome in action of the child's own experience, of his own understanding, of his own ability to look and see. (*Sacred Signs*, pp. 9-12)

Based on this position, Guardini explores some vital facets of the sign language that marks Catholic worship life. Even if I shall abstain from further direct quotes, the following account draws extensively on *Sacred Signs*. The sign of the cross is clearly most important in this connection. Through the cross, God sanctifies all parts of us. This is the reason why we do the sign of the cross at the blessing, in prayer — and when we face temptations. When we bow or kneel, we literally diminish and humble ourselves. This is, therefore, the sign of meekness and modesty. We do this when we enter and leave the house of God, the church; when we pass the Tabernacle — the place of Christ's presence; and above all when bread and wine become the body and blood of Christ in the Eucharist. At the same time, we raise our heads in order to see when the elements are elevated; this is the point of the elevation. Standing is an expression of reverence and alertness. We therefore stand when the gospel is read and when we pray the Eucharistic prayers. In beating our chest — preferably with a notable blow — as in the confession of our sins, we also express humility and ask for pardon. Personally, I would like to add that gospel processions and the priest's kissing of the Lectionary may prove to be just as steadfast a sign of faithfulness to the Scriptures as an increasingly abstract "Scripture alone" principle.

In addition to what we do and the acts we perform, several objects fill the church room and our worship service. According to Guardini, wax candles are reminders that we should become "dissolved" in truth and love of God, in the same way the candle is being evaporated in order to create light and glow. The consecrated water cleans, while at the same time referring to our baptism. When we enter and leave the church, we dip our fingers in this water and make the sign of the cross in order to cleanse our soul. Incense carries the mystery of beauty. It has no distinct purpose, but ascends towards God to his glory. Simultaneously, it symbolizes the love that fervently burns through death, and our prayers that also aim at glorifying the Father through the Son in the Spirit.

In the Eucharist we celebrate the unity with God in Christ that in the final instance is the only thing that can grant human beings peace. This unity is grounded in our eating of the bread that is Christ's body and our drinking of the wine that is his blood. Bread is plain and healthy nourishment. In Guardini's account, it is a sign of the reliable and sustainable. Even if this may not be fully in tune with current slimming regimens, it still makes sense to most of us. Wine is drink and liquid. But it is not just meant to stop our thirst; this is what water does. Hence, wine is not only sensible and simple; it is a symbol of abundance and profusion. And finally, when the grains become one bread and the grapes are gathered in the wine, it witnesses to our communion with God in Christ and with each other. This communion is at the core of our Eucharistic celebration.

Such points are examples of the straightforward and direct nature

116

of the church's sign language. In most cases, this language is accessible to empirical sensation and common sense. Thus, it does not need spiritualized interpretation. At the same time, it takes us into the center of Christian faith. In both these respects, the sign language of worship is essential to a materialist spirituality.

Many regard prayer as a predominantly personal spiritual exercise. This is true, but only partly so. For God's people also pray together, as a body — especially within the framework of our liturgical worship and the office of the hours. Here I once more refer to St. Augustine's claim that those who sing their prayers in the liturgy pray twice as strongly. This shows that the worship service of the church can and should be seen as an act of prayer, ranking among our most central acts in this field. Here we pray through the words of Scripture — like the Psalms and New Testament hymns; here we pray together with and for the whole people of God; and here we pray for the world. In this way, common liturgical prayer is capable of freeing us from the spiritual egoism or the endless circling around ourselves that often sets its mark on our personal prayer life. The Eucharistic prayers are particularly important in this connection. But the collective nature of prayer is also demonstrated when the priest in the Collect of the liturgy "collects" our prayers and includes them in the church's prayer. And when prayers are said responsively, it reflects their dialogical nature. Subsequent to this, the reconciling potential of prayer should be noted. For as St. Cyprian states in a treatise on the Lord's Prayer: God only hears prayers that create peace.

Prayer is absolutely essential to the church and all its members; it is our principal language in addressing God. This language is not constructed for religious insiders. It is neither an abstract and superficially intellectualized entity, nor a spiritualized "prattle" that only a select few can grasp and relate to. St. Augustine maintained that longing is prayer and prayer is longing. Prayer thus expresses our not always fully conscious longing for God — and what we long for, we love. Moreover, the language of praying is grounded in something that is elementary and natural, namely trustful children's talk with their parents. This corresponds with the immediate character of the church's sign language in general, and it even applies in a context where parenthood to some is an ambiguous or problematic entity. When Jesus taught his disciples to

117

pray, there was a strong emphasis on directing our prayers to the God who is our gracious and loving Father — as in the Lord's Prayer. Accordingly, prayer is an integral consequence of our status as children of God.

> "Ask, and it will be given to you; seek, and you will find; knock, and it will be opened to you. For every one who asks receives, and he who seeks finds, and to him who knocks it will be opened. Or what man of you, if his son asks him for bread, will give him a stone? Or if he asks for a fish, will give him a serpent? If you then, who are evil, know how to give good gifts to your children, how much more will your Father who is in heaven give good things to those who ask him!" (Matt. 7:7-11)

God is our Father; our prayers are, therefore, directed to him. Additionally, true prayer always takes place in the name of the Triune God. But it is also possible to pray to God through Mary — she who is the Mother of God — and through the saints. We need the intercessions of the whole communion of saints. The idea behind this is that those who have reached a fuller fellowship with God can pray for us who still remain in the world — or for those who are in purgatory or *limbo*. When the Catholic Church as opposed to some Protestants insists that prayer for the dead is fully possible or even mandatory, it is anchored in God's omnipotence and his steadfast wish that "all men (shall) be saved and . . . come to the knowledge of the truth" (1 Tim. 2:4). This is also a vital aspect of the communion of saints, a communion that exists across the borders of time as well as space.

As a link to God, prayer can be many things. It is both personal and collective. It can come in words or be sung. But it can also be without words, in the form of devout contemplation. Much prayer seems to aim at meticulously informing God about more or less petty details that he probably is already fully familiar with — or at communicating the advanced theological deliberations that lie behind our prayers. Such praying often becomes a monologue instead of what it is meant to be — i.e., a dialogue in which we are obliged to listen to God since he carefully listens to us. As compared to our prayer small-talk, speechless "sighs," silent contemplation or meditation, and ritual recitations that are capable of removing all sorts of "noise" from our minds are beneficial types of prayer. And as already mentioned: Seeing — or gazing at the sacrament — can be praying, too. Furthermore, when we pray, we turn to him who always knows what is best for us. This can be the reason why God sometimes answers prayers in a totally different manner than we expected or would prefer.

Praying should never be applied as a measure to demonstrate our own piousness. Here the prayer of the tax collector is exemplary: ". . . standing far off, (he) would not even lift up his eyes to heaven, but beat his heart, saying 'God, be merciful to me a sinner'" (Luke 18:13). This is also the point when we beat our heart or chest in the liturgy of the Mass, excluding all forms of pious extravaganza. Prayer is a blessing, but it can also be a struggle — just as Jesus struggled in prayer in Gethsemane immediately prior to his crucifixion (cf. Mark 14:32-42). Or to put it in the words of the Norwegian poet Alf Prøysen: We must pray till the knuckles of our hands become white. Here it should be added that prayer can never be used as a way of escaping the duties of our daily lives in God's world. "Pray and work," they said in former times — and did so. Accordingly, prayer and work are two sides of the same coin.

Prayer can be spontaneous. This chiefly applies to emergency situations, but can also occur when we are struck by happiness and gratitude. Yet, spontaneity should not be allowed to rule our prayer life as a whole. Prayer must be integrated into our Christian existence as a regular component; we are called to pray continually or "at all times" (Eph. 6:18). To many of us, this is anything but simple: "You do not have, because you do not ask" — or "you ask and do not receive, because you ask wrongly" (James 4:2-3). I have to admit that this sounds disturbingly familiar. And it suggests that we simply need to be educated in prayer. In this connection, Romano Guardini refers to "a preschool of prayer" that has Holy Scripture and church tradition as its key sources. Here he starts from the observation that prayer is an inner necessity, fulfillment, and grace. But it is a duty and an obligation, too. Hence, we can talk about prayer as an incident, but also as something that requires rehearsal. Guardini continues:

> It is often asserted that true prayer cannot be willed or ordered, but it must flow spontaneously, like water from the spring, from within. If this does not happen, if it does not well up from our innermost being, one had better not pray at all, for forced prayer is untrue and unnatural. [. . .]

119

Undoubtedly, there is a prayer which comes unprompted from within. For instance, some unexpected glad tidings may move a man to give thanks and praise to God; or, when in great distress, he may turn to Him whose love he does not doubt. . . . [Yet,] life and destiny may stand as an impenetrable wall between man and God. The feeling of the holy presence may disappear so completely that man may think he has never experienced it. [On the other hand,] happiness may cause him never to think of God. . . . The dictum that "sorrow teaches people to pray" is only half true, for it is equally true that adversity turns people away from prayer.

Prayer which springs from inner longing must, on the whole, be considered as the exception. Anyone proposing to build his religious life on this foundation would most probably give up prayer altogether. . . . The same would happen to prayer that relied exclusively on inner spontaneity. Anyone who takes his relationship to God seriously soon sees that prayer is not merely an expression of the inner life which will prevail on its own, but is also a service to be performed in faith and obedience. Thus it must be willed and practised. (*Prayer in Practise*, pp. 1-2)

In the wake of this, three things that can be helpful in our efforts to learn how to pray should be briefly mentioned: First, concrete tools like the rosary have proved to be a vital support for many — particularly in improving our concentration. Today similar tools are used in many church traditions. Second, the Orthodox Jesus Prayer may help us to integrate praying in our daily lives — or even in our breathing reflex. It normally goes like this: "Lord Jesus Christ, Son of God, have mercy on me, a sinner." Third, we have the opportunity to both learn from and be carried by the prayers of the church. When we feel so miserable that praying becomes an insurmountable burden, it is reassuring to know that someone out there regularly prays for us even if they may not know us. This is a crucial concern in the faithful prayer service of monastery communities, but also takes place within the liturgical worship of the church.

In this chapter we have noted and recalled that a key point in our liturgical worship is that the outward form is fully capable of carrying inner spiritual substance. In the liturgy, we are also led directly into a service

120

of sharing and love to the benefit of all our fellow human beings and the whole of creation. Further, empirical sensation, physical objects, and concrete acts play vital roles in our worship life and the church's sign language. Accordingly, this language is basically accessible to all and does not require lofty spiritualized interpretations. Prayer is personal as well as collective. It requires specific learning and rehearsal, but can also be natural and effortless — like the language children use when they talk to caring parents. All these aspects are essential to a materialist spirituality. Such piety is therefore a liturgically anchored spirituality.

Literature

Bloom, Anthony. *Living Prayer*, new edition. London: Darton, Longman & Todd, 1980.

Bouyer, Louis. *Life and Liturgy*. London: Sheed & Ward, 1956.

De Clerck, Paul. *L'Intelligence de la Liturgie*. Paris: Cerf, 2000.

Fagerberg, David. *What Is Liturgical Theology? A Study in Methodology*. Collegeville, MN: Liturgical Press, 1992.

Guardini, Romano. *Sacred Signs*. Translated by Grace Branham. St. Louis: Pio Decimo Press, 1956.

———. *Prayer in Practise*. Translated by Prince Leopold of Loewenstein-Wertheim. London: Burns & Oates, 1957.

———. *The Spirit of the Liturgy*. Translated by Ada Lane. New York: Crossroad, 1998.

Jones, Cheslyn, Geoffrey Wainwright, and Edward Yarnold, eds. *The Study of Liturgy*. Oxford: Oxford University Press, 1978.

Kavanagh, Aidan. *On Liturgical Theology*. Collegeville, MN: Liturgical Press, 1992.

Lathrop, Gordon. *Holy Things: Liturgical Theology*. Minneapolis: Augsburg Fortress, 1998.

WORLD AND CULTURE

9 For the Life of the World

An Earthly Spirituality

Throughout history, religion and Christian faith have occasionally functioned as escape routes from the world and reality. Gnosticism insisted that the real God should not be dragged down into the dirty work of creation; this was left to a half-God, a Demiurge. While some mystics had a commitment to the earth, others fled from it. Millenarians were desperate to get away from the world. Nineteenth-century neo-Pietism advocated a deceptively pious Christomonism that led, more or less, to an ignoring of the theology of creation. And within the Catholic Church, massive anti-modernist sentiments pointed in a similar direction. Such attitudes had particularly unhealthy consequences in the area of spirituality — in many cases promoting an abstract, aloof, and self-centered piety.

During the last decades, there has been a growing awareness of the theological importance of the world and the requirement of a corresponding moral practice. But we still struggle to maintain a proper balance in this field. On the one hand, many types of neo-religious market spirituality feature evident Gnostic characteristics — using religion as a tranquilizer that aims at sparing us a painful exposure to the world and reality. Similarly, Christian neo-cons argue that the world should be left in the hands of divinely canonized extreme liberalism. On the other hand, some defend a purely political or secularized position — disregarding the fact that creation can hardly get along without its creator, and downgrading the theology of creation to a solely political matter. Contrary to such ditches, Christian faith insists that we may not be *of* the world, but still find ourselves *in* the world. We therefore need approaches that can keep a sweet taste of heaven and a vigorous scent of earth firmly together.

In my deliberations so far, it has been a recurring theme that the world is not a tactically motivated appendix to theology, but a theological topic in its own right and of fundamental importance. Accordingly, God's world is an integral and indispensable part of Christian faith and not something that merely pertains to its practical horizon. I have further noted that the church's goal is not only that a number of souls shall be saved, but that creation shall be freed from its "bondage to decay" and redeemed (cf. Rom. 8:18-25). In its "fleshiness," the incarnation is the key junction between church and world. Concerns like these are essential to a materialist spirituality. Such piety is lived out within the two closely interrelated spaces of church and world. It is not a cramped "religious" thing, but a truly earthly entity. When Christ offered his body "for the life of the world" (John 6:51), this act is also crucial to our spirituality. Along these lines, I have been trying to correct and deviate from all sorts of escapism — without ending up with biased secularization.

In this connection, the ensuing convictions have played a central role:

- Creation and redemption must be understood as two sides of the same coin.
- The incarnation implies an affirmation of the world and true humanity.
- The Holy Spirit is the Spirit of creation and the grounded wire of our life in Christ.
- The church is the priest of creation, aiming at the world's redemption.
- The world is present in our sacramental celebration through earthly elements.
- The liturgy leads us into a committed service to all our fellow human beings.

Admittedly, my deliberations on these topics have often been far too short. But I have tried to state my views. And it makes little sense to repeat them.

126

There is, however, one essential concern that requires further exploration in this area — namely the moral and ethical as well as the concrete and practical implications of the world's theological relevance. Within the context of a materialist spirituality, this especially actualizes two things: our life in and responsibility for the world and God's creation, and the need of a down-to-earth piety that works where it shall and must work — i.e., in our daily existence. Here huge issues like the balance between social ethics and politics, the interconnection between faith and works, and aspects of Christian vocation ethics pop up. However, I shall only touch these issues briefly. My main intention is to place them within the framework of our quest for a viable spirituality. In the wake of this, the cultural aspects of materialist spirituality and its relationship to art will be discussed — also pertaining to its earthliness.

I shall start by highlighting five fundamental perspectives on Christian ethics. First, such ethics has a passionate, radical, and uncompromising side to it. As Christians and churches, we are called to be "the salt of the earth" and "the light of the world" (Matt. 5:13-14). This obligation is absolutely contrary to all sorts of religious escapism. Salt adds vigor and taste; light shines and enlightens. But salt can lose its power, while light can be hidden. When this happens, we seriously fail the world — which needs both salt and light.

Within the authentic moral tradition of the church, there is a strong emphasis on boundless mercy and charity — in tune with the ideal of loving our neighbors. This is essential in the Sermon on the Mount. We read in Luke:

> ". . . I say to you that hear, Love your enemies, do good to those who hate you, bless those who curse you, pray for those who abuse you. To him who strikes you on the cheek, offer the other also; and from him who takes away your coat do not withhold even your shirt. Give to every one who begs from you; and of him who takes away your goods do not ask them again. And as you wish that men would do to you, do so to them. If you love those who love you, what credit is that to you? For even sinners love those who love them. And if you do good to those who do good to you, what credit is that to you? For even sinners do the same. And if you lend to those from whom you hope to receive, what credit is that to you?

> Even sinners lend to sinners, to receive as much again. But love your
> enemies, and do good, and lend, expecting nothing in return; and
> your reward will be great, and you will be sons of the Most High;
> for he is kind to the ungrateful and the selfish. Be merciful, even as
> your Father is merciful." (Luke 6:27-36)

Some theologians have confined these ideals to the heavenly sphere.
Politicians have been keen to tell us that such thoughts may sound nice,
but would create chaos if we should try to put them into practice —
particularly when they threaten the only "holy cow" that is left in
Northern societies, financial growth. In my view, however, we should
not rule out the possibility that these radical — and in some sense
perhaps naïve — measures possess a significant political potential. At
any rate, they are basically transparent, sensible, and logical in providing
appropriate frames for common human life. Further, opposite attitudes
like selfishness, meanness, and greed are irrational, senseless, and im-
prudent — at least if we examine them closely. And — most danger-
ously, such attitudes are bound to lead to the loss of our souls and our
selves. This applies to us both as individuals and as societies.

Second, this suggests that Christian ethics has a more sober or
down-to-earth side, too. At the core of our moral discourse we find
plain, practical, and realizable ideals that can be integrated into our lives
and will benefit both our neighbors and the world. I have already
quoted the Golden Rule. Even the Beatitudes can be seen as pointing in
this direction — counting as blessed the poor in spirit, those who
mourn, the meek, those who hunger and thirst for righteousness, the
merciful, the pure at heart, the peacemakers (cf. Matt. 5:1-10). In a
time when there has been a surge in soaring "neo-conservative" value-
rhetoric in some Christian groups, this is a vital reminder.

Within the church's moral tradition, there is also a focus on what
we can call less dramatic virtues: In a society where disrespect for human dignity and extravagant flamboyance seem to be joining forces, and
where humility and meekness are mocked, the rekindling of sound *decency* would help us to realize true fellowship and inclusiveness. This is
not a petty bourgeois concern, but a virtue that is grounded in Scripture
— cf. the stories of the good Samaritan (Luke 10:25-37), the prodigal
son (Luke 15:11-32), and the Pharisee and the publican (Luke 18:9-
14). In a world marred by intolerance with racist features, there is a

strong demand for *generosity and open-mindedness*. Qualities like these are also vital to the Catholic vision, aiming at incorporating what is believed everywhere, always, and by everyone. In a situation where egoism and self-sufficiency flourish in our immediate relations as well as internationally, concrete *solidarity and care* are desperately needed. Such ideals are firmly anchored in the incarnation, in Christ's boundless act of solidarity. Further, in a society where grading of human value has spread excessively, commitment to *the equal dignity of all human beings* is a crucial challenge. And in a world where enmity and aggressive hatred spread, we must breed *a spirit of friendship*.

Contributions of ethicists like Emmanuel Levinas ("humanism of the other"), Hans Jonas ("the imperative of responsibility"), and Alasdair MacIntyre ("after virtue") are helpful in developing this approach further. I cannot go into these contributions in detail here. But there has been a growing interest in virtue ethics in recent years, i.e., an ethical approach that focuses on character and personally grounded values. Not all of this is equally good. In a complicated world, we have no guarantee that well-intended ideals will work positively — which suggests that their specific outcome must be critically examined. At the same time, there is a proclivity today to welcome moral approaches as long as they are not costly to us in the sense that they require personal sacrifices. An example of this is that we ask for measures against global warming, but protest vehemently against higher gas prices and air fares. Such double standards demonstrate that we need virtues that are firmly anchored in our personality.

Third, Christian ethics surpasses the sphere of politics, while at the same time having substantial implications in the political field. On the one hand, moral theology deviates from party politics. It also differs from one-sided ideological approaches. On the other hand, Christian social-ethical reflection cannot be limited to delivering general and abstract principles for our life and responsibility in the world. These principles must be concretized. And since we here face challenges with evident political connotations, such concretization will have to be politically relevant and valid. Let me add that Christian virtues like solidarity, sharing, mercy, compassion, and justice are bound to have political consequences in today's world — not least as forceful correctives.

There is a difference between individual faithful and the church when it comes to the level and nature of political concretization. Each

129

Christian is a citizen and a member of civil society. In this capacity, we have duties and tasks that involve voting and party politics. The church, however, is a communion that is basically open to all, regardless of political and ideological attitudes. Yet, there is a limit here — implying that those who adhere to opinions and attitudes that clearly and persistently break with the basics of our moral tradition can face temporary barring or even excommunication. This was actualized when the Lutheran World Federation in the late 1970s opted to exclude member churches that practiced apartheid. Also in regard to political concretization, it must be underscored that Christian ethics does not operate with double moral standards. Even if ethical concerns may look somewhat different in the space of the church than in the life of individual faithful, the same standards apply.

In the wake of this, something must be said about a so-called functionalist ecclesiology. Some may feel that my stressing of the interconnectedness of church and world is in danger of ending up with such a position. Here there is an exaggerated and predominantly pragmatic focus on what the church *does*, on its purely practical functions. However, I would argue that what the church *is*, in its sacramental identity and in accordance with God's calling, is just as important in this connection — in some sense even more important. Or rather: What the church *does* is grounded in what it *is* — not the other way round. At any rate, it cannot be reduced to the level of a mere means in its relationship to the world. But once more, the church is never detached or secluded from the world. The best way of solving this dilemma is to see the church as *sacramentum mundi*, a sacrament in and for the world. A sacrament is never an isolated end in itself. It is an effective sign, a sign that carries its own fulfillment, a "real symbol." This corresponds with the church's role as the priest of creation, the first-fruit of a reunited humankind and a foretaste of God's kingdom. Especially the last of these images is primarily concerned with what the church is — as a sign of the kingdom where the smallest are biggest and the last become the first. In contemporary society, such values possess immense political potential.

Fourth, the social-ethical practice of the church is to a significant degree attached to its diaconal service and its mission as a whole. I have already suggested that the diaconate has two pillars: It is anchored in the liturgy of the Mass and in the church's sending to the world —

hence, providing an essential link between worship and mission. Within the Eucharist, the deacon carries our offertory gifts to the altar in response to Christ's sacrifice. In the immediate continuation of the Mass, he — or she — leads the congregation out in order to serve our neighbors and the world. Here I would like to add briefly that I see no reason why the diaconate should be closed to women. This practice mainly depends on the fact that the present ministry has been considered as a pre-stage of the priesthood. As far as I can gather, such a view neither complies with the diaconate's original character nor with its crucial role in the church's life.

The mission of the church is founded in God's *missio* — or in the Father's sending of the Son and the Holy Spirit. After Christ's ascension, the apostles were entrusted with spreading the gospel of the words and deeds of their Lord. This apostolic sending will continue in the church until Christ returns in order to fulfill his work. Seen in this perspective, mission is a specific function in the sense that it is grounded in and focused on Christ. Still, the church is Christ's body in the world — indicating that every essential part of its life has a missionary dimension. This actually implies that all the chapters of this book are relevant in exploring the mission of the church. Simultaneously, a strong missionary commitment is fundamental to a materialist spirituality. Such spirituality is particularly committed to holding firmly together the preaching of the gospel and our witness to the world through all sorts of diaconal services. Generally, the focus on mission is a forceful corrective over against so-called ecclesiocentrism. This reminds us that the church is no end in itself; it is the priest of creation.

The church's mission must be marked by commitment, but it must also have a widely communicative nature. Approaches with theocratic implications are disastrously incommunicative in today's situation. This, however, does not mean that the church should withdraw from the public space. The noted German philosopher Jürgen Habermas has recently suggested that religious voices can play an important role in the public discourse. He especially emphasizes the capacity of religion to formulate moral positions with a view to collective forms of human life. At the same time, this presupposes that we are able and willing to translate our religious vocabulary into a common language. If not, civil society will be deprived of our insights. This signifies that a communicative dialogue is essential to the public mission of the church.

Fifth, the world in its present, rather shaky state is at the core of our mission. All the problems of the world are our problems; the world's frailty is our frailty. Not least in a time of ecological crisis, this destiny of fellowship should be evident to all. As the priest of creation, the church prays for the world and caters to its needs. At this point, however, it is important to keep in mind that the world has other sides, too. The theology of creation reminds us that the world is not solely a deplorable and pitiful entity. As God's earth, it carries a stunning, almost breathtaking beauty. In essence, this beauty is a reflex of the initial beauty of creation — and, thus, of God. Seen in this perspective, the world also provides an immense positive stimulation in our mission. I can hardly believe that anyone who has had a glimpse of the world's splendor will ever consider fleeing from it. We rather stay on — in stubborn hope and solidarity, waiting for the time when its original beauty will be fully restored.

I have stated that Christian ethics is characterized by specificity and concreteness. Which ethical challenges, then, are most burning in our current social and international context? In a world marked by rapid change and constant fluctuation, this question can hardly be answered by general definitions. In my opinion, however, the so-called JPIC-process of the World Council of Churches from the 1980s is still relevant as an overarching framework. Here the focus is on "Justice, Peace and the Integrity of Creation." This process led to a far stronger emphasis on our responsibility for creation and on environmental or ecological challenges, to a notable degree based on inputs from aboriginal peoples. Another vital presupposition was that the listed tasks were clearly interconnected and could not be separated. Furthermore, the JPIC issues were not optional extras in the church's life, but fundamental concerns.

In today's situation, the JPIC challenges may look a bit different. But there are also evident parallels — not least in the sense that these challenges remain closely interrelated. The call for *justice* commits us on several levels. Here struggle against oppression, racism, and all sorts of discrimination play central roles. Yet, the continual growth in poverty is the key concern in this connection. This is a question of justice and not only of charity. And it would be bluntly ignorant to trust that this acute problem can be solved by the forces of the "free" market. Since the

"Cold War" between East and West more or less has come to an end, we may cling to the illusion that *peace* is not such a vital task anymore. Yet, there has been a surge in new wars — partly due to an increasingly intense pursuit of limited energy resources. Additionally, a huge market for redundant weapons has been created. This shows that the exhortation to "beat our swords into ploughshares" (Isa. 2:4) still applies.

As already indicated, the *environmental problems* are likely to be the most burning issues today. Regrettably, a far too human-centered theology has not been helpful in creating awareness in this field. There is thus a need for a new and dynamic approach to responsible stewardship. It is time to realize that these problems cannot be solved without corporate as well as personal sacrifices and a readiness to change the consumerist lifestyle that is totally dominant in Northern and Western societies. This suggests that the environmental crisis cannot be understood as a disease in nature; it is rather a severe cultural emergency or a problem of cultural mentality. There is no button we can push to halt global warming; it is created by us and can only be stopped by us. Our inability to face the ecological challenges in a convincing way reminds me of the anecdote of the two needles that owned a balloon together. One day they had a quarrel. And then one of the needles said to the other: Hold your tongue, or I will pierce your part of the balloon. . . .

When we participate in the struggle for justice, peace, and the integrity of creation, we are not only facing disastrously destructive forces in the political realm. These forces militate against God's will for the created world; they may even have demonic implications. Accordingly, this is also a question of sin. In this way, it becomes clear that sin is not only a power in our personal lives; it also dwells in political structures. On this basis, we can talk about structural sin. And such sin can only be fought effectively through political measures. This enhances the importance of our social-ethical obligations.

So far, I have tried to present a picture of crucial moral and ethical challenges that face us on a personal as well as a social level. Due to continual changes, this picture is far from complete. But it may provide us with a certain impression of areas that deserve close attention. However, a materialist spirituality stresses the need to transform virtues and values into a sustainable practice. Here the long-standing theological exchange on the relationship between faith and works is highly relevant. Since I cannot go into this huge topic in detail, I shall have to settle with the following brief deliberations.

Faith connects us with the creator. Thus, the world clearly needs faith — even if there is a lack of awareness of this. But the world also desperately needs good works — and that will be more obvious to it. This is the simple reason why works play a key role in our witness to and service in the world, as something that flow from faith. In this sense, faith and works are interrelated. And even if these entities must be differentiated, they should never be torn apart.

This corresponds to the New Testament witness: In Galatians 5:6, circumcision is rejected as a way to salvation, while "faith working in love" is highlighted as a crucial ideal. Similarly in James 2:18: ". . . some will say, 'You have faith and I have works.' Show me your faith apart from your works, and I by my works will show you my faith." First Peter 2:12 affirms that works are particularly important in regard to our witness in the world: "Maintain good conduct among the Gentiles, so that in case they speak against you as wrongdoers, they may see your good deeds and glorify God on the day of visitation." And — even more clearly in Jesus' own words: "Truly, I say to you, as you did it to one of the least of these my brethren, you did it to me" (Matt. 25:40; cf. 25:45). This shows that good works are essential to our faith life. There is only one way that such works can become problematic, i.e., if they are done in order to earn salvation. This is a totally vain project: ". . . no human being will be justified in [God's] sight by works of the law" (Rom. 3:20).

Are we, then, at all capable of doing good works, or have sin and the fall ruled out this possibility? Obviously, sin is an influential power in our lives, and this often means that even our best intentions are mixed with selfish motives. "For I do not do the good I want, but the evil I do not want is what I do" (Rom. 7:19). Here Paul formulates a general human experience. Yet, this does not mean we are unable to do things that are beneficial to others. As human beings, we are not marionettes. After the fall, we can still distinguish between good and evil — and choose the better part. And as we have seen above, Scripture doubtless insists that we are obliged to produce good works.

In the Catholic tradition, however, it is argued that the works we are summoned to do must also be perceived as results of grace. As I have noted earlier, Thomas Aquinas maintains that grace does not annul human nature, but rather perfects it. Through grace Christ works in us and creates new life. This reflects the immense transforming power of grace. What is at stake at this point is not only an abstract declaration from a distant heavenly courtroom that we are counted as justified sinners. Since Christ works both *for* us and *in* us, justification is — primarily — a so-called forensic act through which his righteousness is imputed to us, but it is also an effective process that aims at our sanctification.

This is essential to a materialist spirituality. On the one hand, realism: Nobody can deserve salvation through works; Christ's grace is the only feasible way here. And when Thomas claims that grace is capable of changing human nature, we are not talking about equal partners in the drama of salvation. On the other hand, possibilities: We are both called to and equipped for doing works that are good for the whole of creation. This is grounded in a faith that is shaped by love — having care and solidarity at its core: "Bear one another's burdens, and so fulfill the law of Christ" (Gal. 6:2). If this is ruled out as an option, it is hard to see how a Christian ethics can be conceived at all.

In the wake of this, it must be underscored that neither grace nor justification can be interpreted as static entities. The idea that we over and over again return to an initial state of grace is partly true. Yet, it becomes untrue if it is allowed to conceal that Christian life is also a question of dynamic growth and increasing maturity, just like all forms of human life. This is at the core of our call to holiness. Holiness is never solely our own achievement, but it is always manifested in our lives. We are called to "put on the new nature, created after the likeness of God in true righteousness and holiness" (Eph. 4:24).

I shall not go into the extensive ecumenical dialogue on justification in this connection. As far as I can gather, however, what I have tried to say above is in basic correspondence with the Catholic-Lutheran "Joint Declaration on the Doctrine of Justification" from 1999. This statement is especially important in balancing the forensic and the effective aspects of justification, maintaining that Christ works for us as well as in us. Even if the involved churches still partly disagree on questions like the status of the present doctrine and the relationship between justification and church, this is a highly significant ecumenical step forward. In facing some Lutheran interpretations in this area, one might get an impression that it is "the doctrine of justification" which saves — in a rather abstract manner — and not Christ. The Joint Declaration is helpful in correcting and probably even excluding such approaches. Here it should also be kept in mind that justification is not the sole way to describe salvation in Christ.

Following up on this, I have some brief remarks on the relationship between justification and the church. In the previous chapters of this book, the church has repeatedly been described as the place of salvation. And I have suggested that this is in keeping with the fundamental Article V of the Augsburg Confession. However, this does not mean that justification can be understood as the private deposit or property of the church. What is at stake here is the church as the place where we, through the means of grace and particularly the Eucharist, partake in the fruits of Christ's sacrifice. Arguing that the church in an isolated institutionalized sense can save would be just as senseless as to claim that we are saved by "the doctrine of justification." The church is an efficient sign of the gospel of justifying grace in Christ — and not the other way around. Justification is, therefore, theologically prior to ecclesiology. Simultaneously, the church is the concrete space where justification becomes operative. In this way, the doctrine of justification is liberated from the sphere of abstract ideas; it becomes "flesh." Moreover, it would be rather strange if the church that is Christ's body on earth should be without any role whatsoever in the attribution of salvation. Rather, the church should be seen as the sacrament of salvation. And Christology or the incarnation provides the main link between soteriology — the doctrine of salvation — and ecclesiology — the doctrine of the church.

Finally, and even more importantly in this connection: In justifying us by grace — freely, as a gift, independently of everything in us — Christ also liberates us from meanness, egoism, and selfishness, enabling us to live at peace with God and all people. This corrects our inclination to claim our rights while forgetting our duties to others. As the community of the justified, the church is called to embody the good news that forgiveness is a gift to be received from God and shared with others. Such a church has the capacity of serving as a sign of generosity, solidarity, and reconciliation in a world that desperately needs but acutely lacks such virtues. This is crucial to our mission.

As a part of its ethical commitment, the church must be ready to confront its members with concrete moral obligations that pertain to a Christian life. Here we need churches that are willing and able to speak with a distinct voice — on solidarity and our responsibility to share as well as on topics in sexual ethics. There is much in evidence that we have experienced a decline in consistent moral clarity lately. To a certain extent, this may depend on people's touchiness over against critical perspectives, but it probably also reflects a lack of courage within the churches. In this connection, however, the complicated nature of many ethical challenges must be taken into account. Superficial solutions will always be counterproductive in an ethical perspective. And it is important that the church renounce any biased, judgmental, and condemning approaches.

At this point, it should be reiterated that Christian ethics always is anchored in and aims at reconciliation. Real reconciliation requires repentance. But in human relations, this requirement applies to all parties. Furthermore, the outset and unique foundation here is our reconciliation with God in Christ. However, this crucial fact has immediate consequences on a common human level and in regard to creation as a whole. As it is expressed in the Catholic liturgy of the Mass: "Lord, may this sacrifice, which has made us our peace with you, advance the peace and salvation of all the world" (3rd Eucharistic Prayer). The interconnection between reconciliation in Christ and our ministry of reconciliation in the world is also confirmed in 2 Corinthians 5:17-20:

> . . . if any one is in Christ, he is a new creation; the old has passed away, behold, the new has come. All this is from God, who through Christ reconciled us to himself and gave us the ministry of reconciliation; that is, in Christ God was reconciling the world to himself, not counting their trespasses against them, and entrusting to us the message of reconciliation. So we are ambassadors for Christ, God making his appeal through us. We beseech you on behalf of Christ, be reconciled to God.

At the core of this reconciliatory process, we do not find vague ideas, but a concrete and palpable thing: namely love — primarily God's boundless love to us in Christ, but also our love towards each other, within the framework of a mutually committed fellowship. Not to forget our love of all our fellow human beings and the whole world. This love is not a mere sentiment. It is a bond "which binds everything together in perfect harmony" (Col. 3:14).

Such love is absolutely indispensable to a materialist spirituality. It forms the basis of a spiritual life in solidarity and compassion, generosity and decency, fellowship and friendship: A spirituality that truly aims at the life of the world.

Literature

Cessario, Romanus. *Introduction to Moral Theology.* Washington, DC: Catholic University of America Press, 2001.

Gutierrez, Gustavo. *A Theology of Liberation,* new edition. London: SCM, 2001.

Hauerwas, Stanley. *A Community of Character: Towards a Constructive Christian Social Ethics.* Notre Dame: University of Notre Dame Press, 1981.

Hollenbach, David. *The Common Good and Christian Ethics.* Cambridge: Cambridge University Press, 2002.

Häring, Bernhard. *The Virtues of Authentic Life: A Celebration of Spiritual Maturity.* Liguori, MO: Liguori Publications, 1997.

Jonas, Hans. *The Imperative of Responsibility.* Chicago: University of Chicago Press, 1985.

Levinas, Emmanuel. *Humanism of the Other,* reprint. Champaign: University of Illinois Press, 2006.

MacIntyre, Alasdair. *After Virtue: A Study in Moral Theory,* 3rd revised edition. London: Duckworth, 2007.

Mudge, Lewis S. *The Church as Moral Community: Ecclesiology and Ethics in Ecumenical Debates.* London: Continuum, 1997.

Wallis, Jim. *God's Politics: Why the Right Gets It Wrong and the Left Doesn't Get It.* San Francisco: HarperCollins, 2005.

10 In the Midst of Life

A Spirituality for Reality

Reality is in low esteem these days. Zealously assisted by myriads of trend specialists and image advisers, we have embarked on a hectic "reinvention" or "reconstruction" of our selves and our lives. The concept of reality has been brutally annexed by a "reality-wave" on TV — i.e., a multitude of incredibly banal, pompous, and private "reality-shows" that, paradoxically, take us beyond any conceivable form of reality. This wave is also a sad sign that we live in a time when what used to belong to the private sphere is forced upon us in the public space, while this space is exposed to privatization. Factors like these make me think of the title of a novel by Milan Kundera: "The Unbearable Lightness of Being." All this may be seen as consequences of "the postmodern project."

Moreover, we are overpowered by a Mickey Mouse–like culture, a Disneyland syndrome that filters away critical and realist perspectives and threatens to drown us in "art" comprised largely of shallow stunts. In this situation, critical cultural expressions have been massively marginalized — or swapped for hollow adolescent "irony." We therefore tend to overlook a bundle of things in our present world that are anything but a laughing matter. Even research is exposed to these attitudes, not least in the media-ruled and rather foggy field of "cultural studies." At the same time, densely populist currents have led to reason and common sense being discarded or even despised. The costs of our lost sense of reality are evident — and highly bothersome: superficiality, excessive boasting, the pursuit of comfort and luxury, etc.

This trend has also set its mark on the religious sector. Flamboyant market spiritualities are pungently focused on the selling of exotic and unreal types of religion, turning us into religious tourists. The preachers of prosperity are desperate to choke reality by noise and showiness. Some try to take refuge in the illusory dream world of wild liberalism. Lately, there have been signs of a general revival of religious escapism. And privatization threatens to bereave faith of its essential public role. In this way, we are dragged away from reality.

When faith loses its footing in the real world, it also loses its grip in our daily life. As already indicated, there seems to be a huge demand these days for religion that does not interfere in how we live our lives, and for beliefs that require little or no personal commitment. At any rate, faith that departs from reality must be anchored elsewhere. But as far as I can see, all conceivable alternatives are rather discouraging. And many of them threaten to turn religion into a cabinet of peculiarities in our society.

The following account has one vital intention — namely to actualize a basic and inescapable fact: In the long run, we cannot slip away from reality. Sooner or later it will catch up with us. And we had better be prepared when that happens. This pertains to our faith, too. Since this insistence has been a recurring theme in the previous chapters, it can be dealt with fairly briefly here. However, a crucial concern should be noted at the outset: Materialist spirituality presupposes that sustainable faith will always be directed towards and grounded in not only the world at large, but also our daily existence and present realities. This may sound boring to some. But in the final instance, it is a key task of religion to equip us for our life in the real world. Especially when things become complicated or even terrifying, such an approach will prove to be the only viable form of piety.

The Bible contains several examples of sober, down-to-earth, and realist faith practice. Probably the most startling one is found in the Easter gospel. Having witnessed the earthshaking events of Calvary and the dramatic encounter with the empty grave, the Gospel of John concludes with these laconic words: "Then the disciples went back to their homes" (John 20:10). This suggests that true faith — even after the most shocking upheavals — leads us back to our "homes," that is, to our daily lives and reality. A less escapist attitude can hardly be conceived.

In 1 Timothy, realist faith is applied to the life in the congregation and the Christian existence as a whole: "Have nothing to do with godless and silly myths. Train yourself in godliness; for while bodily training is of some value, godliness is of value in every way, as it holds promise for the present life and also for the life to come" (1 Tim. 4:7-8). Behind this lies one of the first encounters with a Gnostically inclined, escapist, and "odd" religion. Such exhortations also serve as correctives over against Gnostic neo-religiosity today.

Throughout the two letters to the Thessalonians a similar position is advocated, even in facing strong eschatological expectations and currents: Since "the day of the Lord will come like a thief in the night" (1 Thess. 5:2), the faithful are called to remain awake at all times. Yet, this prompts them towards the opposite of escapism: "Rejoice always, pray constantly, give thanks in all circumstances; for this is the will of God in Christ Jesus for you. Do not quench the Spirit, do not despise prophesying, but test everything; hold fast what is good, abstain from every form of evil" (1 Thess. 5:16-22).

Some church members were evidently so preoccupied with the return of Christ that they consistently overlooked their regular duties. Paul brusquely denounces this as "living in idleness" (2 Thess. 3:6). And he adds: "If any one will not work, let him not eat" (2 Thess. 3:10). Furthermore: "Brethren, do not be weary in well-doing" (2 Thess. 3:13). An abandonment of these concerns is incompatible with Christian faith.

It has been suggested that the first Christians expected the immediate return of Jesus, within the framework of a radicalized eschatology. However, even if this should be a correct assumption, within the early church such expectations rarely led to a neglect of daily life and the world. Quite on the contrary, most of the faithful were determined to show that they — in the midst of their commitment — lived a decent and largely ordinary life, a life that did not in any sense represent a threat to the common good. Exaggerated enthusiast attitudes were primarily adopted among the heretics. And these attitudes were already being fought in New Testament times. On this background, the soberness of faith cannot be seen solely as a feature of organized or institutionalized religion.

In the course of the history of theology, these and similar biblical concerns have been further developed. Admittedly, escapist tendencies have emerged, too. Some of these tendencies are mentioned in the pre-

141

vious chapters. Here I would like to add that while authentic pietism was committed to charitable and diaconal work, later neo-pietism adopted a fierce culture-critical view that had seclusionist and sectarian "unworldliness" as its chief outcome. In a more implicit manner, the recent Protestant theological discourse — especially on the European continent — is characterized by a rather abstract approach in which vague and theoretical concepts are emphasized to the disadvantage of the concrete realities of theology.

Yet, currents like these have hardly ever become dominant in the larger picture. In offering examples of a more down-to-earth and sober theology, I will restrict myself to briefly listing a few select factors: Doubtless, the theology of creation has throughout the centuries and in its varying shapes played a most important role in this connection. Within this context, the focus is not only on the world on a macro-level, but also on our daily lives and present realities. Obviously, the world and reality are interconnected concerns.

Lutheran vocational ethics is highly relevant at this point, too. A key presupposition here is that we meet God's claims or his calling to us in our civil vocation and the basic relations of our daily existence. This is the location where we serve both God and our fellow human beings. Accordingly, our Christian calling is realized within the framework of the same relations and vocations. Martin Luther was reluctant to reserve the phenomenon of calling for the religious or ecclesiastical sphere. It just as much pertains to our ordinary life and the public sphere. As already indicated, central aspects of Lutheran vocational ethics have been essential to my outlining of a materialist spirituality.

This approach was further elaborated in twentieth-century Scandinavian Lutheran theology. The Swede Gustaf Wingren insisted that creation and the world are the main arenas of God's calling to us. His Danish colleague K. E. Løgstrup maintained that the implications of a fundamental "ethical demand" were unfolded and communicated through "sovereign expressions of life" in our factual existence. Earlier versions of Lutheran vocation ethics often had evident static features, in the sense that they stressed that Christians should stay put in their vocation and rank within a massively hierarchical society. The Scandinavian contributions are far more dynamic and appropriate to present realities.

Among other positions that have furthered a reality-anchored theology, the Thomist focus on natural law and the common good — *sum-*

mum bonum — could be mentioned. Despite Luther's criticism of the Aristotelian foundation of Thomism and the fact that some of its later versions functioned as "logical" straitjackets, many expressions of this current show parallels to the creation theology of the Reformation. On the more contemporary scene, Christian humanism, so-called grass-roots-theology, and notable parts of the theology of liberation aim at holding together our service in the world with an anchoring in reality and our daily life. And as we have seen in the preceding chapters, Catholic contributions to sacramental theology — such as the description of the church as *sacramentum mundi*, a sacrament in and for the world — have parallel connotations.

How, then, can the interrelation between a reality-focused theology and a materialist spirituality be described in a more specific way? I shall here have to limit myself to the following short points, partly summarizing previous deliberations: First, the real world and our daily lives provide the framework for an encounter with God of significant importance. To a certain extent, this can be seen as similar to God's revelation in creation. This is also the space in which we try to fulfill God's calling in serving our neighbors and the world.

Second, it must be reiterated: A spirituality that does not function where it shall and must function — namely in our daily lives — is of little worth. A spirituality that drags us out of reality is even worse. We therefore need a piety that can provide our faith life with a solid footing. This is one of the key tasks and assets of a materialist spirituality. And it contributes significantly to the concrete embodiment and corporeality of faith.

Third, this does not mean that our spirituality should be totally immersed in or absorbed by our daily existence. In longing patiently for Christ's return in order to fulfill his work, a materialist spirituality also helps us to lift our heads. And it clearly affirms that our spiritual life must include critical approaches. This corresponds to the fact that we are *in* this world, but not *of* it. Once more, a sweet taste of heaven and a sound scent of earth must be kept together.

Fourth, especially in present Western or Northern societies, there is a desperate need of constructive critical perspectives. This is the case in ethical as well as cultural terms. Without such criticism, we will stop growing. And then we may die, at least culturally. The critical potential of a materialist spirituality thus ranks among its most vital assets and must never be forgotten. Here I would even suggest that there is a certain resemblance between this kind of piety and the "critical theory" that was advocated by the Frankfurt School — Theodor Adorno being its chief proponent and even now a highly relevant prophet.

Fifth and finally, it must be stressed that the interconnection between spirituality and reality also works the other way round. Our worship life and liturgies are marked by sustainable reality, too. This is first and foremost the case in their capacity to remind us of a crucial concern: In the long run, the world can hardly get along if its Creator is being disregarded. This is affirmed in our struggle for justice, peace, and the integrity of creation.

In an attempt to exemplify the down-to-earth and reality-bound character of a materialist spirituality, I shall quote from a collection by the Norwegian poet and Lutheran theologian Oskar Stein Bjørlykke. The poems are in a Western Norwegian dialect and not easy to translate. But I have given it a try:

> We don't walk in sight any
> of us. That's true.
>
> But what my eyes got a glimpse of,
> that's what they glimpsed.
> [. . .]
>
> We shouldn't sit on the fence
> waiting for the Kingdom.
>
> There's no meaning to that.
>
> Only when we struggle with what
> is, we can wait for that Kingdom.
> [. . .]
>
> When the sun shines through the colored
> windows in the church, there's
> always such a nice glow.

I like to sit in that glow.

Then I think of the writing above
the door to the choir. It says: *Soli Deo
Gloria*. And there's something to that.
[. . .]

He spoke a lot of law and
gospel, that man. But he
didn't say what everyone knows.

The law is like the biting frost of winter.

And the gospel is like an amazingly
nice snowfall, the day
the air's become milder.
[. . .]

At times we get scared.
That can't be helped.

Then we just have to look straight into emptiness.

But sometimes it seems like
behind emptiness, there it's full.

(Oskar Stein Bjørlykke. *Hans Klure*.
Oslo: Det Norske Samlaget, 1974;
translated with permission by the author)

I do not mean to suggest that a spirituality for daily life must have a
naïve appearance. In my opinion, however, the ponderings of the in-
vented figure Hans Klure have a considerable theological depth to them
— a depth that surpasses abstract theological acrobatics, not to mention
hip but momentary flamboyance. This at least is the case if the intention is to stay grounded in reality, God's reality. And where else can we
human beings be grounded?

One last key point in emphasizing materialist spirituality as a spirituality for our daily existence is to sketch a piety that does not stand

145

and fall with the devoutness we may be able to produce. A spirituality that can be integrated in our lives; that is accessible always and to all; that is anchored in plain acts; that so to speak is embedded in our breathing reflex or our blood; that simply *is* there — independently of us. This is also an expression of grace. When life is at its most miserable, there is not much space for loud and soaring pious exercises. But basic empirical sensation remains a source of communication. Or more precisely: We can "taste and (hopefully!) see that the Lord is good" (Ps. 34:8) — in the Eucharist. And when we feel totally unable to pray, we can gaze at the sacrament and clutch the rosary. This actualizes the pastoral significance and potential of a materialist spirituality. It does not, admittedly, sound terribly "spiritual." Still, it may give us an idea of a viable piety.

Literature

Perhaps a bit typically, reality and our daily lives have not been key concerns in scholarly theology. And the manual-style handbooks on Christian life are often rather shallow. Still, I have tried to think of some contributions that may be helpful here.

Berg, Clayton L., and Paul E. Pretiz. *Spontaneous Combustion: Grass-Roots Christianity, Latin American Style.* Pasadena, CA: William Carey Library Publications, 1996.

Keys, Mary M. *Aquinas, Aristotle, and the Promise of the Common Good.* Cambridge: Cambridge University Press, 2006.

Løgstrup, K. E. *The Ethical Demand.* Notre Dame: University of Notre Dame Press, 1997.

Pannenberg, Wolfhart. *Faith and Reality.* Philadelphia: Westminster John Knox Press, 1977.

Wingren, Gustaf. *Luther on Vocation,* new edition. Eugene, OR: Wipf & Stock, 2004.

11 "The Heart Is Slow to Love What the Eye Does Not See"

The Role of Art in Materialist Spirituality

There are several reasons for including a chapter on culture and the arts in this account of a materialist spirituality. Culture constitutes a fundamental part of the world where such piety is lived out. Cultural and artistic expressions, therefore, contribute significantly to our understanding of and linking to the world. They even have the capacity of lifting the world into our worship and liturgy. In my opinion, this particularly pertains to modern or modernist art. Furthermore, culture and art have — with relatively few exceptions — played a central role in the church's life. This is the case internally as well as with regard to its mission. Today, however, the church tends to be associated primarily with past culture. We thus need to escape from a purely nostalgic approach in this area.

Additionally, it must be underlined that there is an evident link between art and materialist spirituality in the sense that both rely heavily on empirical perception or sensation. In view of art and especially modernist art, this was strongly stressed by John Dewey. And as we have seen in the previous chapters, the same applies to a materialist spirituality. Just as we relate to and grasp artistic expressions through sight and hearing, what we see and hear is essential in our Christian life, too. This also suggests that neither art nor faith can be accessed solely through abstract reflections. I think it was the rock musician Elvis Costello who once suggested that writing on music can be just as meaningless as "dancing on architecture." Seen in a theological perspective, this actualizes the need to connect theology — and particularly ecclesiology — with spirituality.

Such concerns compare to the intention of the title of this chapter. The phrase "the heart is slow to love what the eye does not see" stems from the great Michelangelo. It emphasizes something that is rather obvious, namely the importance of sight in human affection. While not only focusing on outward beauty or prettiness, the point here is simply that what remains distant or foreign may generate admiration and attraction, but it is not easily loved. This is also the case in our relationship with God. Love of God presupposes that he in some way or other comes near to us. This, of course, primarily takes place in Christ. But art is also vital in visualizing the reality of God, if not in the sense of photo snapshots.

It must be admitted, though, that there is a certain ambiguity to the phenomenon of sight in the Christian tradition. According to the Old Testament, human beings cannot bear to see God in his holiness — at least not face to face: ". . . you cannot see my face; for man shall not see me and live" (Exod. 33:20). When God reveals himself, it takes place through means — like a burning bush — or wondrous acts. In some cases, people's eyes are being veiled. This is clearly contrary to today's culture with its strong emphasis on sight and visibility. Not least, television has accustomed us to seeing just about anything in the midst of our living room; we can even watch wars from our armchairs. The Christian version of this habit is to overvisualize faith through spectacular and tremulous feelings. This reminds me once more of Martin Luther's assertion that it is the impious who demand sights, while the truly pious settle for the invisible.

Within the context of the new covenant, this works in a different way. On the one hand, Paul argues that we "walk by faith, not by sight" (2 Cor. 5:7). This statement particularly seeks to correct a piety that aims at false anticipation. On the other hand, Christ is "the image of the invisible God" (Col. 1:15); he is the icon of icons. Now, Luther insisted that even in Christ we only see God from "behind," as he comes to us in Christ's sufferings on the cross. But this too includes a concrete sight. Moreover, "'what no eye has seen nor ear heard' . . . , God has revealed to us through the Spirit" (1 Cor. 2:9-10). And ultimately — when Christ's work is completed and God has become everything to everyone, "we shall see him as he is" (1 John 3:2).

At this point, it must be added that there are spaces where the basic invisibility of faith is transcended, or points where we get glimpses of the invisible realities of faith. This happens within the church, especially in connection with the sacraments or the means of grace. As I have stated several times: In the church we see and hear, taste and smell — through water, bread, wine, and other elements. We even believe that these entities not only allow us to "sense" Christ, but also transform the church into his body and let us partake in his death and resurrection in a very specific manner. Here materialist spirituality really becomes materialist; here it finds its concrete *materia* or stuff.

This corresponds to the church's fundamental visibility. As already indicated, the church may be concealed in the sense that only God knows its true members. But this does not mean that it is invisible. Quite on the contrary, it becomes highly perceptible and palpable through the perceptible and palpable means that constitute it — i.e., word and sacrament. Accordingly, visibility belongs to the church's nature as the place of salvation. In the wake of this, space is provided for other ways of visualizing and manifesting the contents of faith — including art. One of the key tasks of Christian art is to concretize and mediate the image of God that is conveyed through Christ within the church. Thus, it helps us to love God. We might even suggest that artistic expressions have a sacramental character; they become visible signs of the God who surpasses our imagination. At this stage, we have to settle with seeing "in a mirror dimly" (1 Cor. 13:12). But this too is a kind of sight.

Throughout the church's history, art has played a central, if somewhat varying role. Already in the Old Church, such expressions were important in articulating and communicating the gospel — chiefly by symbols and basic imagery. There was a marked setback in this area in connection with the iconoclastic struggles, mainly during the eighth century. In the end, however, the impressive icon theology of the Eastern tradition and a viable icon spirituality triumphed. From the ninth century, different art forms were essential to Christian worship. During the high Middle Ages, the church became both the most important art patron and the chief arena for displaying art. A major part of all the art that was created in this period had a Christian aim and content. This was primarily the case in the fields of music, visual arts, and architecture, but partly also in literature and drama. Further, much of this artistic output was clearly groundbreaking, innovative, and renewing. While the patron function increasingly was taken over by courts and the nobility in the

West, the church's dominant role continued well into the fifteenth century in the Byzantine Empire.

I cannot go into the vast and fascinating subject of icons in detail here. Together with impressive mosaics, these images played the leading role in the flourishing Byzantine Christian art. Even if icons mainly portray Christ, the Virgin, the saints, and central events in salvation history and church tradition, they may even symbolize the Holy Trinity — as in one of Andrej Rublev's most famous contributions to the genre. Icons are seen as carrying what they depict in a direct manner. They are, therefore, objects of veneration. While the iconoclasts denounced iconic imagery as a form of idolatry, the Council of Nicea in 787 maintained that the honor that is paid to the image passes on to the person in the image — implying that it is the person, and not the image, that is venerated. An icon-based spirituality soon became a key feature in Eastern Orthodox life, in an ecclesial as well as a personal perspective. This kind of piety has several points of resemblance with a materialist spirituality.

In many ways, the Reformation led to a notable change in the attitude to art. Martin Luther was deeply and genuinely fond of music. And he promoted a strong renewal in the hymn tradition of the congregation, if not so much in its liturgical life. Yet, even music was attributed with a predominantly instrumental function here. Basically, all sorts of Christian art were understood as tools for what the Reformers saw as the paramount concern, namely the supreme preaching of the gospel. Art was therefore placed at the level of religious pedagogics; it was considered primarily as secondary illustration of the biblical message. And the artistic expressions were perceived as means — or even crutches — for the gospel. Now, Luther ended up by opposing the radical Reformers and the fierce iconoclasm of Andreas Karlstadt. But it has been argued that there are more or less explicit lines from his instrumental approach in the area of art to an iconoclastic practice. In any case, the results of the militant radical Reformation can still be witnessed in churches across the European continent, in the form of badly smeared pictures of the Holy Virgin and decapitated statues of the saints. These deeds are also signs of aggressive anti-Catholicism.

As far as I can gather, aspects of the "aesthetics of means" or the instrumentalized aesthetics of the Reformation are still clearly influential. In some churches, the instrumental view has been fused with dense populism. Here cultural contributions are not only perceived as plain illustrations of the gospel, but also as tools for popular self-expression and self-realization — almost in line with the dreadful "Idol"-shows on TV. Hence, we are overpowered by culture that works in private living rooms, but hardly in the public space. The inescapable result of this is a church culture that lacks both artistic value and cultural sustainability. Such practices are frequently grounded in an evasive and almost self-destructively populist folk-church idea in which the church largely is understood as the property of the people. And like all forms of populism, the Christian version too is directed towards delivering static affirmations — it is a culture that hardly ever challenges, and thus fails to promote growth.

The Roman Catholic attitude to culture in general and modern art in particular has been highly ambivalent. Throughout the nineteenth century and even up till the Second Vatican Council, the church was marked by massively anti-modernist views — resembling the fiercely cultural-critical position of radical neo-pietism. At the same time, the contours of a Catholic modernity grew forth before and after the Second World War, especially in France. Here names like Georges Bernanos and François Mauriac, Georges Rouault and Françis Poulenc, Léon Bloy and Jacques Maritain played central roles. The most important theological contributions to this movement came from the Dominican Marie-Alain Couturier, who coined the slogan: poetry rather than pedagogics. This heritage was later taken up and further developed by Olivier Messiaen, perhaps the greatest composer of the twentieth century, who was both densely modernist and densely Catholic. In a typical statement, Messiaen maintained that he preferred to be seen as "a liturgical functionary" and not as "a mystical composer." In another contribution I have described Messiaen's music as an expression of a "baptized modernism."

Much remains to be done in regard to the attitude and practice of the Catholic Church in the field of culture and arts. Sadly, premodern sentiments seem to be gaining ground today. Still, the Protestant "aesthetics of means" never became so dominating within the church, mainly because the Catholic focus on sacramentality provided space for the conviction that Christian art had its own inherent value beyond the level of pure means. In my opinion, there is even a certain similarity between a sacramental understanding of art and the modernist concept *l'art pour l'art* — art for its own sake and on its own premises. The church's openness to modernist art expressions is reflected in the fine Vatican Museum collection of modern art that was initiated by Pope Paul VI — also in this sense emerging as "the first modern pope." And John Paul II published "A Letter to the Artists" in 1999.

Art is capable of stimulating, invigorating, and energizing the life of the church and our spirituality. It further adds a healthy and robust earthliness to faith. And it contributes notably in establishing a bridge to or a meeting point with the world. Religiosity without art tends to come across as sterile and barren. Accordingly, the church desperately needs art. The rather austere results of approaches that "divorce art and religion" are expressed in "Bleak Liturgies," a poem by the Welsh poet and Anglican priest, R. S. Thomas:

> Instead of the altar
> the pulpit. Instead
> of the bread the fraction
> of the language. And God
> a shadow of himself
> on a blank wall. Their prayers
> are a passing of hands
> over their brows as though
> in an effort to wipe sin
> off. Their buildings
> are in praise of concrete
> and macadam. Frowning
> upon divorce, they divorce
> art and religion.
> Ah, if one flower
> had been allowed to grow
> between the wall
> and the railings as sacrament
> of renewal. Instead
> two cypresses ail
> there, emaciated as the bodies
> of thieves upon Calvary
> but with no Saviour between them.

(Mass for Hard Times, p. 59)

Regular iconoclasm hardly exists anymore, except in some densely Protestant or wildly populist versions. There is, however, a disturbing lack of consciousness within many churches in regard to the role and potential of art — not to mention its sacramental promise. Such unconsciousness can be spotted in church interiors, but it can also set its mark on the church's culture and its life as a whole. At any rate, this is yet another example of the gloomy consequences of "(divorcing) art and religion." And if such attitudes are not counteracted, they will continue to block our access to a constructive theological aesthetics.

What kind of art, then, do we need in the church today? In addressing this huge question, personal likes and dislikes will evidently play a certain role. Yet, this vital challenge cannot be solved on the basis of mere "taste" or what we immediately "like." An appropriate response here requires cultural and aesthetic insights as well as relevant theological reflection. In my opinion, much of contemporary church culture has been caught in the backwaters of market-sensitive populism and stagnant nostalgicism. The following considerations may be helpful in trying to escape from this dead-end:

First, there is a demand for art that can reflect the stunning beauty of God and his creation. Yet, the gospel affirms that the path to life goes through death. This indicates that divine beauty transcends the level of one-dimensional cuteness and pleasantries. It also deviates significantly from the worshiping of superficial splendor and the pomposity of some types of bourgeois aesthetics, despite the fact that such positions often have had a strong influence on our theological aesthetic deliberations. God's beauty includes humility and meekness; it may even encompass aspects that in some sense appear as awful or hideous. And it is firmly focused on the most beautiful thing that can be envisioned — i.e., the story of Christ, the one who gives his life for the many. This story is breathtakingly beautiful. But it clearly surpasses outer prettiness and the merely picturesque. All this points towards what Michelangelo characterized as "the other beauty," a beauty that rests in God. In securing a proper balance in this area, the theology of Hans Urs von Balthasar can be fruitful. Let me add here that there is a limit to how many times the Christian message can be coupled with harmonizing cultural expressions like, say, Charles Gounod's rather sweetish *Ave Maria*, without being deprived of its power.

Second, as an inclusive community the church needs art with broad appeal and accessibility — steering clear of snobbishness and arrogance. At the same time, this concern must not be allowed to lead to massive cultural populism in line with a purely instrumentalized aesthetics. As already mentioned, populist culture is bent on delivering static affirmation — shunning critical approaches and thus depriving us of possibilities of cultural and human growth. This is an obvious dead-end within the church. We must seek vibrant and radical art, cultural expressions that can free us from drowsiness and apathy — in line with what was said about the general requirement of critical culture in the previous chapter. Furthermore, art with a broad appeal should not be taken to mean mediocrity in terms of quality. Here I would like to refer to Theodor Adorno's important observation that canonization of mediocrity necessarily leads to veneration of the cheap. In more practical terms, the requirement of cultural sustainability and persistency is especially important in the church's life. This is not least due to frequent repetition. Seen in this perspective, the increase of so-called praise songs with ten notes and not much more than ten words must be critically examined. Such songs are in many cases examples of what happens when quality is sacrificed to the benefit of instant popular appeal.

Third, we still need art that can visualize, articulate, and interpret the gospel as well as central parts of the history of salvation and the Christian tradition. And we need music that can express and accompany the offer of praise that we are obliged to bring forth in response to Christ and his boundless sacrifice on the cross. However, we cannot settle with a plainly illustrative function at this point, let alone with mere repetition. We must, therefore, look to art that has the capacity of stimulating imagination and creativity in our encounter with the gospel. Art has a special potential in providing us with new perspectives on and angles to the ancient message of the church. In this way, ever more of the gospel's immense richness will be opened up to us.

Fourth, there is a demand for culture and artistic expressions that reflect and mediate God's real presence among us through Christ in the Holy Spirit, and the deep comfort this presence gives. This is crucial to the mentioned sacramental character of Christian art. However, we also require artistic expressions that mirror the nagging feeling that God is absent in the world and in the lives of human beings. The distress and desperation that this sentiment frequently leads to must be voiced, too. There is much evidence that such devastating feelings are widespread in today's world, even if we regularly try to escape from them through denial or noise. But they are rarely articulated in an explicit way within the church that is sent to serve the world.

Fifth, continuity is essential in a church that largely lives from old stories and traditions, and where we believe together with those who went before us. Accordingly, a lack of a sense of history is just as bothersome in Christian culture as in church life as a whole. Yet, continuity is not the same as retrospective nostalgia. It would have damaging consequences if we should fill the church with "gregorianic light" or endless repetitions of old prayer-house songs. This would turn it into a cabinet of rarities or a mausoleum of the past. The church would thus be stripped of significance in regard to present realities and our factual lives — confining them to indifference or oblivion. Our efforts to secure a balance between continuity and renewal may take an assertion that stems from Bernard Lonergan as their point of departure: Any present is powerful to the extent that past experience lives on in it. This reflects the value of previous lessons in shaping the future. However, within the bounds of pure nostalgicism there is no future to be shaped; there is just a flight back into "the good old days." Such escapism is anything but helpful in the life of a church that is called to serve the world and all human beings. What we need here is continuity-based renewal, or a renewal that is grounded in continuity. In the wake of this, openness to non-Western cultures is an important concern.

Personally, I have had a special interest in the place and role of modernist or classical modern culture in church life. This culture grew forth at the end of the nineteenth century and during the first half of the twentieth. In breaking with traditional tonality and favoring abstraction in visual arts as well as a free style in poetry, it represented a cultural renewal with shocking implications to many. And it still has the capacity of shaking us in our drowsiness and complacency. Cultural modernism is a predominantly Western phenomenon. But it was also inspired by impulses from other continents, such as African sculptures, Latin American murals, and so-called aboriginal art.

I shall not go into the value and promise of modernist culture in detail in this connection. My intention is just to indicate briefly some aspects of this type of culture that may have special relevance to the church. At first it should be underlined that many Christian adaptations to cultural modernism correct the impression that modernity and classic Christianity are mutually excluding entities. I have already mentioned the uncompromisingly modernist music and the largely traditional Catholic faith of Olivier Messiaen. The architect Antoni Gaudì even aspires for sainthood; a formal process aiming at his beatification will possibly be opened up. The Norwegian composer Fartein Valen — often referred to as the fourth member of the Second Vienna School — had little or no affinity to the Catholic tradition. All his life he was anchored in a typically Western Norwegian neo-pietism. Yet, he was just as committed to modernism as Messiaen in the music he wrote. Here we see few if any signs of the cleansed Romantic "artist religion" that was favored by a number of poets and composers during the nineteenth century. And while considerable parts of theology have had huge difficulties in connecting modernity and classic faith, all these artists — and quite a few more — offer evidence that this is not at all impossible.

Simultaneously, it is a myth that modernist artists generally denounced religion. Arnold Schönberg's music was inspired by both his Jewish roots and the tradition of the church. Vasilij Kandinskij remained committed to Christian ideas and concerns, not least in his account of the "spiritual" aspects of visual arts. And in the field of literature, a vast number of modernist writers drew more or less explicitly from the Christian tradition. This is yet another affirmation of the links between cultural modernism and Christianity.

Theodor Adorno argued that only modernist music — particularly as expressed in the works of the three great figures of the Second Vienna School, Arnold Schönberg, Alban Berg, and Anton Webern — was able to voice the sufferings of modern human beings in an authentic way. This potential is of immense theological relevance. In my view, modernist culture has the capacity of lifting the world — in its terrific beauty as well as its desperate agony — into the church's worship and its life as a whole. And such presence is absolutely essential to the people of God; without it we simply cannot celebrate the Mass in spirit and truth. Generally, this actualizes a highly important task of culture within the space of the church. It cannot settle with reflecting the gospel in a narrow sense; it shall also serve as a concrete and inescapable reminder of and representation of God's world. One of the key tasks of art is to provide a defense for vulnerable human beings and true humanity. At this point, I would like to add that modern culture can help us to translate the gospel into a common language.

156

According to Roland Barthes, being modern implies a knowledge of what cannot be repeated anymore. Such knowledge is vital to a church that is sent to serve the world in its present shape. However, an awareness of what remains viable and sustainable is also required here. Older art or art that has survived throughout the centuries is often, if not always, good art; and good art will never lose its relevance. An example of this can be found in the music of Giovanni Pierluigi da Palestrina, the leading composer of the Catholic Counter-Reformation. Together with Johann Sebastian Bach, Palestrina and his counterpoint provided a fundamental source of inspiration to several modernist composers. In the final instance, what the church really needs in this field is *true* culture — new as well as old. And true culture is basically anchored in reality.

I started this chapter by referring to Michelangelo's assertion that "the heart is slow to love what the eye does not see" — being most relevant in regard to a materialist spirituality. I shall now conclude with a similar, positively directed affirmation from an artist in the modern tradition — namely the famous, and in some respects quite notorious, English sculptor Eric Gill. The Stations of the Cross in Westminster Cathedral in London is one of his central works. In 1913, Gill was received into the full fellowship of the Roman Catholic Church. He reflects on the key reasons of his decision to convert in a later biographical note:

> I would not have anyone think that I became a Catholic (only) because I was convinced by the truth. I became a Catholic because I fell in love with the truth. And love is an experience. I saw. I heard. I felt. I tasted. I touched. And that is what lovers do.
>
> And lest anyone should think that in this devotion to the Mass, to the Blessed Sacrament, to the Holy Eucharist I am devoted to an abstraction, to a purely intellectual and even aesthetic Catholicism (not that such things are to be despised or rejected) I must say this: the Real Presence which we affirm is the real presence of the man Jesus.
>
> Let no one suppose that because we adore him in spirit we do not adore him in our hearts. Very God, yes. And dear Jesus also. He speaks to us and we speak to him. We kiss the hem of his garment, we also thank him for bread and butter.
>
> He ordained that our bodily motions should be pleasant and grat-

ifying and that the pleasure of marriage should be beyond the dreams of avarice. He ordained the thunderstorms and the lion's voracity; he also blesses the daisies and the poor. He sits in judgement; he is also friend and brother.

This account corresponds directly with the key concerns of a materialist spirituality. Here we recognize the emphasis on empirical sensation, on the fundamental concreteness of faith, on the outward sacramental signs and especially the Eucharist, on the true humanity of Jesus, and on creation in its beauty and truth. Gill did not solely talk about these things. He first and foremost mediated them through his art. And that took place in a very explicit manner, speaking more accurately than loads of abstract ideas.

Along these lines, it is reaffirmed that art is crucial to our spiritual life. This is based on its imagining, concretizing, and communicative potential. By making God close to us, art really helps us to love him. At the same time, modern or modernist culture in particular contributes to renewal and a sound anchoring in the real world. The sacramental character or promise of art is thus substantiated. And no church can afford to disregard this promise.

Literature

Adorno, Theodor W. *Aesthetic Theory*, new edition. London: Continuum, 2004.

von Balthasar, Hans Urs. *Seeing the Form: Glory of the Lord. A Theological Aesthetics*, vol. 1. Fort Collins, CO: Ignatius Press, 1982.

Bourdieu, Pierre. *Distinction: A Social Critique of the Judgement of Taste*, new edition. London: Routledge, 1986.

Brown, Frank Burch. *Religious Aesthetics: A Theological Study of Making and Meaning*. Princeton: Princeton University Press, 1989.

———. *Good Taste, Bad Taste, and Christian Taste: Aesthetics in Religious Life*. New York: Oxford University Press, 2000.

Dewey, John. *Art as Experience*, new edition. New York: Perigee Books/ Penguin, 1980.

Gay, Peter. *Modernism: The Lure of Heresy: From Baudelaire to Beckett and Beyond*. New York: W. W. Norton, 2008.

Lossky, Vladimir, and Leonid Ouspensky. *The Meaning of Icons*, 2nd revised edition. Crestwood, NY: St. Vladimir's Seminary Press, 1983.

Rössler, Almut. *Contributions to the Spiritual World of Olivier Messiaen, with Original Texts by the Composer.* Duisburg: Gilles & Francke Verlag, 1986.

Thomas, R. S. *Mass for Hard Times.* Newcastle: Bloodaxe Books, 1992.

Welsch, Wolfgang. *Grenzgänge der Ästhetik.* Stuttgart: Reclam, 1996.

FURTHER EXPLORATIONS

12 "No Man Is an Island"

An Ecumenically Based Community Spirituality

The worst thing is to be left in solitude, say those who have lost their spouse or someone close to them. *You'll never walk alone,* the fans or the famous Kop at Anfield football stadium in Liverpool shouts. Or as the English poet and priest John Donne wrote roughly 400 years ago: *No man is an island.*

> All mankind is of one author, and is one volume. . . .
> [. . .]
> No man is an island, entire of itself.
> Every man is a piece of the continent, a part of the main.
> (from *Devotions upon Emergent Occasions,*
> *Meditation XVII*)

Human beings are not created to live in splendid isolation, as hermits or deeply incurved on themselves. The longing for community lies in our nature. And even if we occasionally may need a break from socializing, most of us dread loneliness.

Still, fellowship has become increasingly hard to find, especially among those who need it most. The welfare state is under severe pressure, even if we know that it is very difficult to rebuild structures of security and common care when they have been dismantled. Personal compassion seems to be vanishing. Neo-liberalists claim that we should manage on our own, in keeping with their previously favored litany-*less* state. . . . An example of this attitude can be found in a depressing but typical utterance by former British Prime Minister Margaret Thatcher: "There is no such thing as society." At the same time, basic human relations are jeopardized. And when loneliness and isolation spread, the result will often be growth in anti-social behavior that also imperils fellowship. Additionally, whatever one might think about the phenomenon of "globalization," it has not proved convincingly beneficial in shaping an international spirit of community.

In several respects, religion is an answer to our longing for fellowship. This clearly applies to the Christian faith. "None of us lives to himself, and none of us dies to himself," Paul insists (Rom. 14:7). Further, the church is the body of Christ, a living organism where all members are summoned to serve the whole and the community (cf. 1 Cor. 12). Accordingly, solidarity, compassion, and care belong inherently to its life: "Bear one another's burdens, and so fulfill the law of Christ" (Gal. 6:2). Here solidarity is not only a political concern, but something that is deeply grounded in the core of faith: "For you know the grace of our Lord Jesus Christ, that though he was rich, yet for your sake he became poor, so that by his poverty you might become rich" (2 Cor. 8:9). An essential feature of the fellowship of the church is that all unwarranted or artificial human borderlines are transgressed within it:

> . . . for in Christ Jesus you are all sons of God through faith. For as many of you as were baptized into Christ have put on Christ. There is neither Jew nor Greek, there is neither slave nor free, there is neither male nor female; for you are all one in Christ Jesus. (Gal. 3:26-28)

This potential is rare in a society where a majority of the free institutions and associations are focused on the common interests of ever narrower groups. Regrettably, it has not always been fully realized within the church. But it remains as a promise, as something we at least occasionally can witness.

In exploring the fellowship dimension of the church's life further, the so-called ecclesiology of communion is highly important. This ecclesiology has several ecumenical implications. One of its basic presuppositions is that the church does not only *have* communion among several other assets; it *is* communion. Living fellowship thus belongs to its nature. This is in keeping with the first ecclesial mark of the Nicene Creed — oneness. A church that fails in building and maintaining sustainable fellowship can be seen as more dead than alive. And since it breaks with God's will for the church, unnecessary division is sinful.

The communion of the church goes far beyond our daily horizon. It is grounded in our communion with the Father through the Son in the Holy Spirit. Here we are not talking about a restrained relationship at respectful distance; it implies a concrete participation in and with the Triune God. The goal of our fellowship with God is that all who are in Christ shall "become partakers of the divine nature" (2 Peter 1:4). Or — to express it through the words of St. Athanasius: God has become man in order that man shall become God.

As an immediate and necessary consequence of our communion with God, we also have fellowship with one another. This fellowship stretches back in time. Within the church, we stand together with the faithful who went before us. In our worship we even join in their heavenly praise: "Amen! Blessing and glory and wisdom and thanksgiving and honor and power and might be to our God for ever and ever! Amen" (Rev. 7:12). However, our communion exists across space, too. It is a human fellowship that embraces all who confess Jesus throughout the world. Their faith is our faith, their life is our life, their worries are our worries, and their joy is our joy. In practice, this fellowship finds its most concrete and direct expression in our closer human relations — mainly within the context of the local church and our local community.

This points towards the church as *communio sanctorum*, the communion of saints. What is at stake here is a fellowship with our sisters and brothers in Christ of all times, in each and every place, and in our present local setting. The constituents of this fellowship are holy because they belong to God and are his people. Our holiness is primarily realized through word and sacraments; they are the means that God applies when he sanctifies his people. Therefore, the communion of saints is a communion of human beings who gather around holy things — or, conversely, a communion in holy things that gather a holy people. This community is also summoned to live a holy life, in keeping with God's good will for the whole of creation. Accordingly, the world is the central arena of our call to holiness — and not some secluded religious sector.

In the wake of this, a brief word on saints and their role in the church is apposite. These persons are special manifestations of the power of God's grace. A saint is a sign of the wondrous things that can happen when Christ is at work in the lives of weak and feeble people. The saints also provide us with viable role models in our faith life. They are in a sense like the best in the class, the fellow pupils that we have much to learn from. We really need models of how a holy life can and should be lived, not least in times when such models have become increasingly scarce in our immediate surroundings. This explains why the saints deserve our veneration and why we ask for their prayers.

The communion of the church has our *koinonia* or concrete participation with the Father through the Son in the Holy Spirit as its foundation and core. But love can be seen as the structuring principle of our fellowship. Divine love has the capacity of breeding and releasing human love: "By this we know love, that [Jesus] laid down his life for us; and we ought to lay down our lives for the brethren" (1 John 3:16). Moreover, our community in Christ grows when faith and hope become effective in love. Transforming sacramental grace is crucial to this process. The same is faith formed by love and love formed by faith. True love breeds true freedom. However, love can also be described as a bond, the bond "which binds everything together in perfect harmony" (Col. 3:14). This suggests that mutual love is the glue of our communion. Without it, the fellowship dimension of the church becomes an abstract idea.

All the above-mentioned concerns of the ecclesiology of communion are vital to a materialist spirituality. It has a vertical or Trinitarian anchoring; it is attached to a specific and essentially visible human fellowship — coming across as community spirituality; and it emphasizes love as an indispensable part of the life of this fellowship. In the following, I shall look more closely at some other aspects and implications of the church's nature as communion.

The church *is* communion. This means that all central aspects of its life are lived out in communion. Faith is a personal thing in the sense that it must somehow be anchored in our personality. At the same time, we believe as a body — being manifested in a particular way when we confess our faith together, with one voice, in the Creed. The church is capable of sustaining, supplementing, and completing our faith. It can even in a certain sense believe in our place or on our behalf, especially in periods when we struggle with severe doubt. However, the *communio*

166

life of the church must always be anchored in a shared faith. Today, people tend to look to the church for social fellowship as such. In a society where community bonds are vanishing, this is understandable. It must be emphasized, though, that fellowship within the church is based on unity in faith. And if faith is stripped of its meaning and contents, it cannot function as an effective bond of community.

Yet, this does not mean that our fellowship in Christ is a fellowship in meanings and opinions. The church is not an association for people who share religious tenets and views. Just as faith and life belong together, our communion in faith will always be a communion in life as a whole. Here virtues like human solidarity, compassion, and care play key roles. Our fellowship in life even carries through death. This affirms Christ's victory over death.

As a communion of life, the church is also a fellowship in the life-giving sacraments. We are incorporated into this fellowship through baptism. And when we eat the flesh of Christ and drink his blood in the Eucharist, we — the church — become his body on earth. Also this part of our community has a social dimension. As mentioned previously, Paul criticizes the faithful in Corinth heavily for their failure to account for this dimension, particularly with regard to the so-called agape meal that took place in connection with the Eucharist:

> . . . in the following instructions I do not commend you, because when you come together it is not for the better but for the worse. For, in the first place, when you assemble as a church, I hear that there are divisions among you; and I partly believe it, for there must be factions among you in order that those who are genuine among you may be recognized. When you meet together, it is not the Lord's supper that you eat. For in eating, each one goes ahead with his own meal, and one is hungry and another is drunk. What! Do you not have houses to eat and drink in? Or do you despise the church of God and humiliate those who have nothing? What shall I say to you? Shall I commend you in this? No, I will not.
> [. . .]
> Whoever . . . eats the bread or drinks the cup of the Lord in an unworthy manner will be guilty of profaning the body and blood of the Lord. Let a man examine himself, and so eat of the bread and drink of the cup. For any one who eats and drinks without discern-

ing the body eats and drinks judgment upon himself. (1 Cor. 11:17-22, 27-29)

The point here is not the social dimension as such, but rather that the lack of social awareness disguises and undermines the sacrament. In this way, our obligation to sharing and justice is enhanced. What Paul actually says is that the Eucharist cannot be celebrated appropriately without mutual love.

The ministries of the church are important in maintaining and visualizing community within God's people, too. In this connection, we are not talking about massive hierarchical structures, but persons who have been endowed with and equipped for special responsibilities and tasks within the body of Christ. The point is simply that a functioning church fellowship needs functioning spiritual leadership. There are many examples that churches that possess such leadership have an enormous potential — regardless of how wanting they may be in terms of material resources. On the other hand, churches that lack distinct leadership may be exposed to damaging developments — despite affluence in other respects. Today, religious privatization, along with other factors, has made it extremely difficult to provide viable leadership in the church.

Ecclesial leadership cannot be exercised above the heads of the believers. It requires the consent of the faithful — *sensus fidelium* — as well as structures for fruitful cooperation. This actualizes the intention of the priesthood of baptized believers. We are all priests, meaning that we have free access to the Father through the Son. Thus, mediating institutions like the sacrificial priesthood of the old covenant are largely redundant. At the same time, there is a difference and a distribution of tasks between the so-called common priesthood and the ordained ministers of the church. These entities must never be confused. If that happens, the outcome will easily be chaos within the body of Christ caused by a situation in which all members want to do the same things. Generally, the ordained ministers are called to serve the fellowship of the church in its totality. They should therefore be seen as a support in our faith life and not an impediment.

The priest is the leader of the local congregation, on behalf of the bishop. Accordingly, he is in charge of the preaching of the gospel and the administering of the sacraments. This does not imply that the means of grace so to speak are the private property of the ordained priesthood. Quite on the contrary, the priest is responsible for preventing individuals and separate groups from annexing what belongs to everybody. Together with the deacons, the priests also lead the sending and mission of the local congregation in the world.

The office of the bishop is a vital bond of unity within the church. Bishops act as successors of the apostles, with apostolic authority. Furthermore, they represent the local church universally, and the universal church at the local level. The unifying potential of the episcopal office is visualized in a special manner when the bishop celebrates the Eucharist in the local cathedral, together with the priests, and in the midst of the faithful. Today, dioceses have regrettably often become far too big to secure and express the original meaning of episcopacy — threatening to reduce this crucial ministry to an administrative function.

According to the Roman Catholic understanding, the Pope — or more accurately, the Bishop of Rome — exercises leadership within the universal church. As the successor of Peter, care for the proper balance between unity and diversity is at the core of his ministry. The papal ministry must be implemented in close cooperation with the bishops. This actualizes the demand of structures for episcopal collegiality within the church. The Pope is also our *papa* — our father in faith. In today's situation, we clearly need such fatherhood.

A materialist spirituality welcomes the services of the ordained ministries with gratitude. Such spirituality deviates from individualizing and privatizing attitudes. And it realizes that structures that contribute to holding the body of the church and its members together are beneficial. This is a question of order and orderly conduct. But it is also a question of solidarity and love.

The concept of catholicity is vital in our efforts to account for the community dimension of church life. The church is one and catholic in its nature. However, catholicity does not mean plain commonness or folksy ordinariness. Neither can it be understood primarily as the name of one church tradition, let alone as the private property of such a tradition. The Roman Catholic Church sees itself as the chief expression of the one Church of Christ, without being identical with the true church in an exclusive manner. Therefore, René Beaupère is correct in arguing that the reunited church lies beyond all present ecclesial realities. The catholicity concept directs us, rather, towards a body that exists "over the whole" — i.e., in all places, across time as well as space. In accordance with Vincent of Lérins's definition, a truly catholic church is supposed to encompass what is believed everywhere, always, and by everyone. A first requirement here is a substantial amount of human generosity. A second requirement is that the rapidly vanishing ability to have two thoughts in one's mind at the same time be kept intact. In my opinion, generosity and openness are essential to the catholic vision.

Second, catholicity demands a proper balance between unity and diversity in the church's life. As Blaise Pascal put it: Unity without diversity is tyranny, while diversity without unity leads to confusion. On the one hand, unity is not the same as uniformity. Quite on the contrary, fruitful diversity belongs intrinsically to unity. Furthermore, diversity cannot be understood as a mere practical or tactical concern. In reflecting God's many gifts to his people in the Holy Spirit, it is an entity of crucial theological and ecclesiological significance. And none of us — let alone no church — can afford to disregard any of these gifts. Generally, diversity is primarily a benefit and not a threat in the church's life.

On the other hand, ecclesial diversity is never a static entity. Accordingly, it deviates from versions of postmodern pluralism where most things are perceived as equally valid. True church diversity is always thus construed as growing towards greater unity. Or more precisely: We grow together towards the fullness in Christ. This growth takes place within the framework of Christ's body, where all members are obliged to serve each other and the community as a whole. Our unity is given in Christ and anchored in God's unity. Hence, nothing in this world can ever overthrow it. For "there is one body and one Spirit, just as you were called to the one hope that belongs to your call, one Lord, one faith, one baptism, one God and Father of us all, who is above all and through all and in all" (Eph. 4:4-6). This affirms that unity belongs to the church's nature. And it indicates that our task is not to create unity on our own, but rather to visualize our given unity in Christ in order that the world may see and believe.

Third, a proper balance between unity and diversity requires a properly balanced relationship between center and periphery in the universe of faith. These two dimensions should not be played off against each other. The doctrine of the church is an organic whole also in the sense that its articles are clearly interconnected. If one truth falls, others tend to follow suit. Moreover, history teaches us that unrestricted pluralism at the core of faith may have devastating consequences. Still, there must be space for fruitful diversity on other questions. Today, the relationship between center and periphery often appears to be turned upside down. This is the case when some press for uniformity on more marginal issues of order, while opting for confusing plurality in regard to the basics of faith. Here the vital Catholic ideal of firmness in the center, flexibility in the periphery, and love in everything is actualized. In all our care for church doctrine, we are summoned to "(speak) the truth in love" (Eph. 4:15).

The church is called to be a sign of unity and fellowship in our local society and the world at large. Ecumenism cannot be seen as an internal concern, but directs us towards the *oikumene* — the whole inhabited world. As the priest of creation and the first-fruit of a reunited humankind, the church is sent with a mission to build community and promote reconciliation everywhere. This task also presupposes a properly balanced relationship between unity and diversity. In our present societies, there are quests for unity that border on oppression and may even have bluntly racist connotations. In confronting such attitudes, we are challenged not only to passively tolerate, but to actively embrace and rejoice in diversity. Here generosity and openness are indispensable virtues.

This is clearly relevant in regard to immigration policy and attitudes towards minorities. It makes little sense to welcome people from other cultures, while expecting them to become like us overnight. In many circles, it has become fashionable to complain that multiculturalism is a threat to our tradition, religion, and customs. I would rather argue that such presence represents an immense source of enrichment. And it would be gratifying if more energy had been put into this promise than in preventing Muslim girls from wearing their *hijab*. At the core of racism is fear. And fear can only be conquered through real knowledge. The churches should, therefore, contribute in providing meeting places where we can learn about each other, and thus learn from each other.

At the same time, our obligation to unity remains the key challenge in this field. We live in a world marked by division and strife on just about every level — between poor and rich, women and men, young and old, etc. Basic human relations are seriously jeopardized, and the number of violent conflicts and warlike actions keep increasing.

171

There is a desperate demand for institutions and persons that are able to demonstrate, through visible evidence and concrete deeds, that healing and reconciliation can still be achieved.

This is a vital task for the Christian community. Admittedly, parts of our practice here may be inadequate. Still, the church exists in all parts of the world and has the capacity to transcend unwarranted human borders. This can even be experienced in tiny and rather self-sufficient Norway. In St. Swithun's Catholic Church in Stavanger, people from all over the world, from a vast number of nations and from many different cultures, meet in every Mass. This encounter is not entirely free of tension. Yet, we are effectively united in the liturgy and the Eucharist. We share the peace with joy. We aim at carrying each other's burdens. We try to be receptive to all that we can learn from each other. And we are summoned to witness to unity and fellowship in the world. On the background of this capacity, Jürgen Habermas has recently suggested that the Roman Catholic Church has special potential in the perspective of globalization.

At the core of this obligation is the unity that the creator envisioned for his creation. Unity is a mark of the church. But this does not apply in a narrow or reclusive sense. The mark of unity is only fully realized when we stand forth as a sign of fellowship in and for the world. Among deprived people, lack of care and compassion may have life-threatening consequences. In the case of lonely persons, the outcome may be boundless misery. Even among the affluent, the absence of meaningful relationships may lead to an agonizing feeling of emptiness. Or — as a Norwegian artist put it: People today have got everything, but that is all they have got. . . . Challenges like these are essential to the church. In the final instance, they can only be met through concrete and viable solidarity. However, in Christ we do not face these huge tasks empty-handed. For through his sacrifice, he has reconciled us with God. And he has called us to and equipped us for the grand ministry of reconciliation. There is hardly anything a militantly divided and unreconciled world needs more than this.

The main concern of this chapter is community spirituality in a general sense. Yet, the deliberations above are to a notable degree ecumenically based and — hopefully also — ecumenically relevant. This is not the place to enter into a comprehensive discussion on ecumenical theology as such; I have written extensively on this topic elsewhere. There are, however, evident points of connection between a materialist spirituality and ecumenism that should be considered more explicitly. Here the following issues merit closer attention:

Materialist spirituality is community spirituality; it is, therefore, also an ecumenically grounded and intended spirituality. More specifically, a materialist piety draws heavily on ecumenical theology in general and the ecclesiology of communion in particular. At the same time, such spirituality will be most helpful in putting the fellowship dimension of ecumenism into concrete practice. This actualizes a dialectic that is advantageous to both these entities. In the present ecumenical situation, there has been a tendency to pile up abstract agreements that are not converted into real and living fellowship. A materialist spirituality that is construed as community spirituality represents an important resource in this area; it is an impetus to ecumenical reception. One might even suggest that community spirituality is practiced ecumenism.

Subsequently, materialist spirituality is not minimalist or reductionist. Quite on the contrary, it is eager to draw from the richness of the church's faith deposit in its totality. As already pointed out, there is perhaps not that much which *must* be believed within the fellowship of the church, but there is much which *can* and *should* be believed — simply because it will make our faith life significantly richer. Ecumenism offers by far the best entrance to the abundance of our faith treasure. Here we are reminded that we always have much to learn from the witness of our Christian sisters and brothers. This especially applies to spirituality and how our life in Christ should be lived out in the world. In former times, such learning in most cases was passed from the North to the South. Today, however, this stream should be turned around — actually, it has largely been reversed already. The stronghold of Christianity is rapidly changing. While the churches in the South experience strong growth, the mainline churches of the North are losing members. This shift is also due to the spiritual resources of the Southern churches. There can be no doubt that we in the northern hemisphere have much to learn from these churches. Generally, a materialist spirituality aims at being ecumenically open and relevant. It thus provides a suitable framework for mutual ecumenical learning. Proposals for community spirituality that lack an ecumenical basis will hardly be viable.

So-called *spiritual ecumenism* is essential to the ecumenical venture, particularly on the Roman Catholic side. This type of ecumenism is pertinent to our spiritual life, too. In the Decree on Ecumenism from the Second Vatican Council, it is described along these lines:

> There can be no ecumenism worthy of the name without a change of heart. For it is from renewal of the inner life of our minds, from self-denial and an unrestricted love that desires of unity take their rise and develop in a mature way. We should therefore pray to the Holy Spirit for the grace to be genuinely self-denying, humble and gentle in the service of others, and to have an attitude of brotherly generosity towards them. . . . So we humbly beg pardon of God and our separated brethren, just as we forgive them that trespass against us. . . . All the faithful should remember that the more effort they make to live holier lives according to the Gospel, the better they will further Christian unity and put it into practice. For the closer their union with the Father, the Word, and the Spirit, the more deeply and easily will they be able to grow in mutual brotherly love. . . . This change of heart and holiness of life, along with public and private prayer for the unity of Christians, should be regarded as the soul of the whole ecumenical movement and merits the name "spiritual ecumenism." (*Unitatis Redintegratio;* nos. 7-8)

At the time of the Council, this reflection was in many respects groundbreaking — also in a wider perspective. Later on, Pope John Paul II spoke about ecumenism as a mutual sharing of spiritual gifts. Spiritual ecumenism has a number of crucial implications: It shows that the desire for unity is located at the core of our faith. It emphasizes the need of repentance, holiness, and renewal as ecumenical virtues. It distinguishes ecumenism from mere ecclesial diplomacy. It provides space for common prayer for and other public manifestations of fellowship. Finally, it is a fundamental principle of spiritual ecumenism that the closer we get to God in Christ, the closer we will also get to each other.

However, as much as I welcome these concerns, there are some catches here. The first one is represented by a tendency to regard spiritual ecumenism as an alternative or even a substitute to doctrinal ecumenism — i.e., as something we may revert to in troubled times, such as the present "ecumenical winter." Accordingly, it is important to emphasize that these approaches must be seen as two sides of the same coin or as complementary angles. This implies that spiritual ecumenism by necessity requires committed efforts to solve our doctrinal controversies — and vice versa. If this dialectic is ignored, spiritual ecumenism may well degenerate into a *"spiritualized* ecumenism."* And this will be just as counterproductive as all kinds of Gnostically inclined notions. Additionally, we have noticed that the concept of "spirituality" frequently comes across as problematic or blurred today. This depends primarily on the fact that the present entity has been turned into a commodity in an increasingly colorful — one could even say kitschy — religious market.

With this in mind, one might suggest that there are good chances of a positive interaction between spiritual ecumenism and materialist spirituality. While the first stresses the ecumenical dimension in general and essential virtues like contrition and meekness, a materialist piety offers a firm foundation in reality and sound critical perspectives. Hence, a spiritual ecumenism that is kept together with a materialist spirituality may appear as more concrete and palpable; while a materialist spirituality that is associated with spiritual ecumenism will increase its ecumenical credibility and potential.

All these observations confirm that materialist spirituality and ecumenism are mutually complementary entities. Both approaches aim at embracing the vast richness of Christian faith; they are anchored in solidarity and sharing; and their goal is to realize community. They are crucial in regard to the inner life of the church, but never stop with this. Thus seen, ecumenism as well as a materialist spirituality will be capable of contributing something that both the church and the world desperately need — namely, sustainable fellowship.

Literature

Bonhoeffer, Dietrich. *Sanctorum Communio: A Theological Study of the Sociology of the Church*, new edition. Minneapolis: Augsburg Fortress, 1998.

Hortulanus, Roelof, Anja Machielse, and Ludwien Meeuwesen, eds. *Social Isolation in Modern Society*. London: Routledge, 2005.

Kasper, Walter. *A Handbook of Spiritual Ecumenism*. New York: New City Press, 2007.

Meyer, Harding. *That All May Be One: Perceptions and Models of Ecumenicity*. Grand Rapids: Eerdmans, 1999.

Tillard, Jean-Marie. *Church of Churches: The Ecclesiology of Communion.* Collegeville, MN: Liturgical Press, 1992.

In regard to challenges facing Roman Catholic ecumenism in the present situation, I would like to refer to this article:

Tjørhom, Ola. "An 'Ecumenical Winter'? Challenges in Contemporary Catholic Ecumenism," *The Heythrop Journal* 48, no. 5 (September 2008): 841ff.

13 The Fundamental Reasonability of Faith

Sober Spirituality

I hope this does not sound too conceited. But I cannot help interpreting recent developments in regard to the place and role of rationality in our present society along lines like these: In former times, blunt foolishness was normally seen as a rather discomfiting occurrence, and sound reasoning was widely respected. Today, however, obtuse and trivial considerations are announced from the rooftops, without the slightest sign of embarrassment. Not least on the media scene, perpetrators exceed each other in posing as agents of stupidity. Popular and populist versions of so-called postmodernism provide the framework here. At the core of these currents we rarely find legitimate skepticism in view of the limits of reason, but regular — and often quite unbearable — silliness.

Religion is particularly exposed in this connection. This is affirmed by all types of fundamentalism, with their militant insistence on one-dimensional and simple solutions. But it also applies to the strange mixture of trivial and bizarre elements that mark significant parts of neo-religiosity. Furthermore, what the prophets of prosperity are selling may be understood as a kind of streetwise stupidity. And neo-charismatics prefer noise and commotion to sense and soundness. The outcome of these approaches is that religion at best will come across as banal, at worst as plain alchemy. This makes me think of an apposite statement by the Catholic Norwegian author and Nobel Prize laureate Sigrid Undset: Faith surpasses reason, but it also surpasses our feelings.

The aim of this short chapter is not to discuss the intricate relationship between faith and reason in a wider perspective. My intention is only to substantiate that materialist spirituality is a sober spirituality capable of accounting for the basic reasonability of faith. Here it should be recalled that soberness is a biblical virtue: ". . . let us keep awake and be sober" (1 Thess. 5:6). However, materialist piety must also somehow be grounded in reason. Only in this way can it shield us from flamboyant senselessness.

In order to clarify my point here, I shall start with a very brief look at how the relationship between faith and reason has been understood. Classic Christianity has largely resisted the pressure from irrational and unreal religiosity. Several of the great theologians of the Old Church rank among the most erudite persons of their time. The ontological argument in favor of God's existence as it was set forth by Anselm of Canterbury still makes sense: God is the highest being; but someone who is present only as concept or idea and not in reality is not the highest being; accordingly, God must exist. Thomas Aquinas succeeded in establishing an impressive synthesis in maintaining that there is an interconnection between empirical sensing and our perception of God. In spite of differences, Martin Luther's creation theology leads in a similar direction. More recently, scholars like Charles Taylor and Wolfhart Pannenberg have contributed to a constructive dialogue between modernity and theology. This must not be forgotten in a time when so-called creationism is surging.

However, there are dead-ends in this field, too. One such dead-end is the bluntly rationalist theology of the late eighteenth century, with its attempts to present a religion cleansed of "superstition." The same was the case with later positions that aimed at harmonizing theological reflection with abstract speculation, positivist attitudes, or naturalism. A constructive relationship between faith and reason presupposes that the validity and integrity of faith are respected. This has become increasingly difficult during the last centuries.

I also have to admit that I have some doubts in regard to the favorite thinker of classic continental European Protestantism, Immanuel Kant, in this field. Kant placed himself between rationalism and empiricism. While criticizing ontological and metaphysical approaches, he also argued that empirical perception was incapable of capturing things as they really are *(Ding an sich)*; it only provided knowledge on how things come across for the observing person *(Ding für mich)*. Theoretical reason was considered as an instrument to organize and interpret what we sense. In the wake of this, Kant tried to sketch a "religion within the boundaries of pure reason." This form of religion did not supply real insights on God and the world, but was chiefly seen as having ethical significance or seen as an appendix to our moral consciousness. One of its central goals was to ensure that virtue and happiness would finally go together, while the existence of God could neither be proved nor invalidated.

On the one hand, Kant doubtless wanted to grant religion a proper space within the universe of Enlightenment. He was committed to religious morals in a traditional sense. And his stressing of the interrelation between religion and moral behavior is important to a materialist spirituality. Yet, Kant shared the pietistic conviction that God's will — in a somewhat "puritan" sense — is at the core of Christian life. Moreover, his ethicized religion and rationalized, rather barren image of God reveals implicit similarities with Protestant iconoclasm. Here God is primarily present through or as moral obligations, not as a living person with whom we can have concrete communion. In the course of time, Kant's emphasis on the dialectic between reason and empirical sensation led to religion being referred — or confined — to the empty "holes" that were left when different types of science had done their job. And as human knowledge expanded, the number of such holes decreased. Eventually, Friedrich Schleiermacher described religion as *Gefühl* — feeling. The result of this development was an internalized, personalized, and privatized belief. The idea that faith could provide us with real insights on the world was dismissed. And religion was left as a largely anthropologized and marginalized entity.

In my opinion, the creation theology of the Reformation and the assertion of Thomas Aquinas that God's existence is open to empirical sensation represent far better options in this connection. Especially since Kant, developments in the philosophy of perception and epistemology have placed theology in a kind of "perceptionist Babylonian captivity" where it is assumed that faith is unable to provide valid knowledge on how the world "really" is. In the present situation, we are facing a massive hermeneutical hegemony. Here everything tends to become a question of interpretation and not of inherent "truth." Thomist approaches may still be useful in freeing theological reflection from such straightjackets. Generally, a theology that admits it has little or nothing to say about "reality" will inevitably be confined to an increasingly diffuse, foggy, and cramped sphere of internalized feelings. Similarly, a theology that accepts its inability to speak about God's creation in a real sense will effectively marginalize itself.

In the wake of this, we shall take a very brief look at the interconnection between human perception and theological reflection as Thomas Aquinas sees it. His starting point is that God's essence cannot be perceived through a mere mental vision *(visione imaginaria)*, but requires concrete forms or signs that represent him. These forms and creation as a whole are effects of God; they can, therefore, show us the creator. Their promise as such effects has been restored through the purification and renewal of creation that lies inherent in the incarnation of Christ. According to Thomas, there is a "hierarchy of perception" here. This implies that lower things are capable of revealing higher things; we can access infinite spiritual truths through finite physical objects.

On this basis, Thomas held that God can be recognized through and in things, signs, and acts that are open to empirical perception — with a particular focus on basic matters that are accessible to everyone. Here there is no need for an inner spiritual illumination as Augustine claimed; the "natural light" that all human beings possess is sufficient. Such views did not lead to arrogance; meekness remained a central virtue to the "angelic doctor" of the church. In the theology of Thomas Aquinas, sight *(visio)* plays a key role — not in the form of internalized visions, but as concrete imagination: To become a believer is to become a seer. The peak of imagination is attached to the elevation of the sacrament in the Eucharist, as expressed in his Eucharistic hymns. Additional visible signs and acts within the context of our worship life follow suit. Another well-known expression of Thomas's approach to empirical perception and theological reflection is found in his argument in favor of God's existence: On the basis of factual movements in nature, the presence of a first mover — namely God — can be deduced, etc. Today, such reflections will not suffice as hard evidence or scientific proof, but they offer a fruitful starting point for meditation on the reality of God grounded in imagination. They also help us to maintain that we can learn about creation through the creator — and vice versa.

Thomism has been crucial to Catholic theology ever since the lifetime of Aquinas. Admittedly, this kind of theological reflection departed notably from its originator when it degenerated into a rigid, reclusive, and self-supplying "logical" system during the nineteenth and early twentieth century — also labeled as neo-Scholasticism. Later, however, Thomism was substantially renewed. I cannot go into this development in detail here. The so-called existential Thomism of Étienne Gilson and Jacques Maritain was vital in this connection. But the transcendental Thomism of Joseph Maréchal, Karl Rahner, and Bernard Lonergan is probably even more important in the perspective of renewal. Within this current it is a key presupposition that we can know the finite only if we know the infinite. To a certain extent, this provides space for impulses from the transcendental method of Kant and Kantianism. At any rate, such approaches show that at present Thomism cannot be associated solely with restorative and retrospective positions. In my view, they demonstrate that Thomist theology and perception theory still are supremely valid angles.

Thomism is clearly relevant from the perspective of a materialist spirituality and its foundation in regard to its original shape as well as several of its more contemporary versions. And this is especially true of its attempts to hold empirical perception and rationality together. Here we are facing a highly beneficial dialectic, demonstrated by the following three examples:

First, both Thomism and a materialist spirituality are firmly grounded in empirical perception. In this area, creation and worship life, observations in nature and liturgical acts are of crucial importance. Theologically speaking, such perception is far more "reliable" than sterile logics. One might also refer to John Locke's insistence that nothing enters our reason without already having been in our perception. Yet, there is an interaction between empirics and reasoning. Reason is essential in organizing and interpreting empirical sensation. Thus, these two approaches must not be played off against each other, but kept together. Here we have much to learn from Thomas as well as Kant. The Psalms too offer examples of deduction from creation and human life to God: "For as the heavens are high above the earth, so great is his steadfast love toward those who fear him; as far as the east is from the west, so far does he remove our transgressions from us" (Ps. 103:11-12). To a materialist piety, the progress from creation to the creator and then back again to creation plays a key role.

181

Second, materialist spirituality is conceived as a widely understandable and accessible piety. It is "democratic" and open to all in the sense that it does not require a special religious antenna system. Also in this field, plain empirical sensation and sound reasoning are highly important resources. As Jürgen Habermas insists, religious faith must be communicable in a commonly comprehensible language in order to become meaningful to society at large. Within this framework, empirics and reason will even be of significance in regard to the church's mission. In this connection, the capability of dialectical reasoning and the readiness to have several thoughts in mind simultaneously will be clearly helpful, while one-sidedness and single-mindedness are dead-ends. As suggested by the late Norwegian Lutheran bishop Eivind Berggrav, it would be rather sad if only the one-eyed were reckoned to be seeing.

Third, materialist spirituality is a down-to-earth piety that remains steadily anchored in reality. It therefore departs from the neo-religious propensity towards unreal religion and religious tourism. Such religiosity requires a rationally based critique. Once more, the interaction between empirical sensation and reason emerges as a fundamental asset. What is at stake here is not abstract and elusive theories, but rather sober reasonability — or solid common sense. Empirical perception has proved to be helpful in providing lofty and secluded speculations with a firm footing in reality. In this connection, differing philosophical currents like phenomenology, radical empiricism, and pragmatism may also have quite a lot to contribute.

The key point of my deliberations above has been that reason and sober sensibility are essential to theological reflection in general and a materialist spirituality in particular. In concluding, it must be stated that this at the outset applies to forms of reasoning that are willing and able to provide room for the faith dimension. And belief differs from reason. Yet, we cannot claim space for a faith that is bent on irrationality and senselessness. It must also be realized that in demanding such space, we have to accept that reason remains reason. It makes little sense to try to turn this entity into some kind of supra-rationalist hybrid. Here there is a need for generosity and openness on both sides. Faith must make it clear to reason that creation cannot be fully grasped if the creator is neglected. At the same time, methods anchored in empirics and reasonability are crucial in handling all sorts of knowledge, including our perception of God. This suggests that faith and reason can be seen as complementary ways to God. Faith has the priority, without excluding rational reflection and empirics. Surely, God surpasses all reason. And revelation often transcends the laws of nature. But this does not mean that our God-given ability to think is annulled.

In order to concretize the interaction between faith and reason along somewhat different lines, I conclude with a quote from Father Brown in one of the short stories of G. K. Chesterton:

> It's the first effect of not believing in God that you lose your common sense and can't see things as they are. Anything that anybody talks about, and says there's a good deal in it, extends itself indefinitely like a vista in a nightmare. And a dog is an omen, and a cat is a mystery, and a pig is a mascot, and a beetle is a scarab, calling up all the menagerie of polytheism from Egypt and old India; Dog Anubis and great green-eyed Pasht and all the holy howling Bulls of Bashan; reeling back to the bestial gods of the beginning, escaping into elephants and snakes and crocodiles; and all because you are frightened of four words: "He was made Man."

> (G.K. Chesterton,
> *The Incredulity of Father Brown,* 1926)

This is typically Chesterton — and perhaps not entirely conversant today. But surely, the coupling of common sense, faith, and the incarnation still seems rather convincing — at least to me.

Literature

Brown, Stephen F., ed. *Aquinas: On Faith and Reason.* Indianapolis: Hackett, 1999.

Habermas, Jürgen, and Joseph Ratzinger. *Dialektik der Säkularisierung: Über Vernunft und Religion.* Freiburg: Herder, 2005.

Kerr, Ian. *After Aquinas: Versions of Thomism.* Oxford: Blackwell, 2002.

McCabe, Herbert. *Faith and Reason.* Edited and introduced by Brian Davies. London: Continuum, 2007.

Taylor, Charles. *Modern Social Imaginaries.* Durham, NC: Duke University Press, 2005.

14 Materialist Spirituality and World Religions

Common Concerns

Throughout the preceding chapters, I have expressed critical views on so-called neo-religiosity — with a particular emphasis on the most market-sensitive versions of this kind of religion and Christian adaptations to its central concerns. Before I finish, however, it must be underlined that this criticism does not apply to world religions like Islam, Judaism, Hinduism, and Buddhism, or to various forms of native religion. Here there are very good possibilities of an open and constructive dialogue. In this connection, materialist spirituality provides an important angle. As I shall try to show in the following, such spirituality plays a key role in most or even all world religions. There are, thus, notable parallels — mainly formally, but also in terms of contents — between the ways in which we worship. As we have seen previously, this is not the case with regard to neo-religiosity — regularly coming across as abstract, fluffy, and rather "unreal." In this very brief chapter, I shall not discuss the theology of religion in a more comprehensive way. My sole intention is to point at materialist spirituality as a link and foundation for dialogue between the traditional world religions. However, this is a particularly vital concern — not least in the present situation.

Even a quick look at the world religions confirms that worship attached to and expressed through basic acts and physical objects in a sacred space is of crucial significance. This is even a stronger feature here than in parts of the Christian tradition — especially in the West, where the abstraction and internalization of religion that took place in the wake of the Enlightenment have had notable influence. The interrelation between religion and real life is also essential in the world religions. They are in most cases expressions of community religiosity. And there is a concern for a suffering humankind and a wounded world.

Due to strong ethnic ties, some may argue that Judaism cannot be seen as a world religion. However, it merits special attention in our context because of its central role in the shaping of Christianity. This especially applies to the church's worship life. Significant parts of our worship can hardly be understood if its roots in Judaism are ignored. Particularly in the perspective of a materialist spirituality, there are numerous parallels here. The meaning of liturgy as a concrete memorial or making present the central events of salvation history is vital to both traditions; Christian acts of and attitudes to prayer are embedded in the Jewish tradition; the great Passover or *Pesach* meal exposes evident similarities with our celebration of the Eucharist; there are connecting links between Jewish life rituals like circumcision, the bar mitzvah — the ritual for coming of age — marriage and death and the sacraments of the church; the dignity accorded to the scrolls of the Torah — the five Books of Moses — reminds us of our gospel processions, etc. Here it can be added that harvest festivals serve as expressions of gratitude and care for the earth within Judaism as well as Christianity. And while public prayer takes place in a consecrated house or space — the synagogue — the Jewish cycle reminds us of our liturgical year.

Despite present political tensions, Islam too shares roots with Judaism and Christianity. This includes concrete acts like washing, bowing in prayer, and practices in reciting and listening to God's word. Even if there is a focus on simplicity and the attentive reading of the Qur'an here, a comprehensive system of rituals has been developed within Islam. These rites are partly anchored in a ritualization of acts by the Prophet Muhammad and other central figures. And they reflect the importance of empirical perception as well as the central place of the body. The five pillars of Islam are: The belief in the oneness of God as expressed in the declaration of the Creed (the *Shahada*); commitment to daily prayer (the *Salat*); almsgiving and care for the needy (the *Zakat*); purification through fasting during the month of *Ramadan* (the *Sawm*); and pilgrimage to *Makkah* (the *Hajj*) for those who are able to realize this. All these pillars display a very concrete and practical form of religion. Furthermore, presence in the mosque on Fridays for common prayer is stressed as obligatory. And there is a strong focus on the interconnection between faith and people's daily existence; the message of the Qur'an shall be lived out in a specific manner in the world.

Within both Judaism and Islam, the role of religious rituals not only in public or organized worship but also in daily life is emphasized. Here not least the family provides a vital framework for living out religious faith. This suggests that Christians have much to learn from Muslims and Jews in integrating religion in our existence as a whole. For Judaism and Islam, the belief in God's transcendence implies a rejection of images of the Divine. However, this rarely led to puritan iconoclasm, but in most cases to other types of religious imagery that can be stunningly beautiful. The spectacular mosaics of the mosques are the preeminent examples of this. Another example is found in the elaborately decorated Torah scrolls with their binders, cases, and crowns. All these things can be seen as expressions of a different kind of iconography.

In Hinduism a host of religious rituals and ceremonies are observed within the framework of concrete acts. Here such rituals are regarded as basic to the maintenance of the cosmos as well as to human relationships, implying a more or less constant interaction with omnipresent gods. Especially as expressed in the teachings of the Buddha, Buddhism to a notable degree started off as a critical reaction against Hindu ritualism. Fairly soon, however, Buddhist ceremonies with monks playing a key role were developed, and the use of images of the Buddha for devotion purposes spread. Subsequent to this, physical objects became central in Buddhist worship, too. Among Hindus as well as Buddhists, external rituals are frequently combined with internal meditation techniques. Within different forms of native religion, rituals and religious acts are strongly focused on the earth — often according it with divine status.

The intention of the account above is not only to point at phenomenological or formal parallels between a materialist spirituality grounded in the Christian tradition and the worship life of other world religions. In my opinion, these similarities also provide us with a solid basis for our interfaith dialogue. Religious sign-languages are largely accessible to adherents of most types of religion. Moreover, all forms of materialist piety are open to empirical sensation, anchored in plain human expressions, and therefore immediate and generally perceptible. Such commonalities will also be helpful in understanding each other across religious barriers, even within a wider human context. This is an example of the potential of religion in promoting mutual understanding.

The dialogue with other religions requires an approach that is both theologically sustainable and sufficiently open in regard to the integrity of our dialogue partners. Here we are facing a dilemma that is indicated already in 1 Timothy 2:3-6. On the one hand, these verses affirm that God "desires all men to be saved." On the other hand, "there is one God, and there is one mediator between God and men, the man Christ Jesus." While the first of these two assertions reflects what can be described as a universalist attitude, the second may at first sight appear as particularist. One tries to solve this dilemma along three main lines: While "exclusivism" stresses that Christ is the only way to salvation, a "pluralist" view is primarily concerned with God's universal will of salvation. There is, however, a third option — often described as "inclusivism." In this connection, it is maintained that Christ is indispensable in the process of salvation. Yet, Christ's work cannot be confined to individual souls. There is a universal dimension to it; it is exercised within a cosmic framework and aims at the redemption of the whole of creation.

This suggests that an exclusivist and a pluralist position can be linked. And the link is actually found in exclusivism itself, i.e., in the cosmic and universal range of the work of Christ. This points towards a kind of "inclusive exclusivism" or "exclusive inclusivism." Here the key concern is that Christ's work of salvation has a wider range and is capable of carrying far more than we tend to believe. In the wake of this, the interrelation between Christian faith and other religions can be understood in light of the figure of several concentric circles that have Christ as their common core. Similarly, the church is both the fellowship of the faithful and the priest of creation. The "normal" seen from our point of view is that we become partakers in the fruits of Christ's sacrifice within the space of the church. But God is omnipotent; everything is possible for him. He can save whomever he wills whenever and wherever he wills. Accordingly, it is possible to maintain that baptism is necessary for salvation, without claiming that everyone who has not been baptized will automatically and irreversibly be lost.

An "inclusivist" position is in keeping with central concerns of a materialist spirituality. And it has significant implications in view of our relationship with other religions. At the outset, we are obliged to fight for religious liberty in all situations. It is also our task to correct increasingly widespread prejudices, misconceptions, and fear in this field. Another obligation is to have deep respect for other religions — not only as cultural phenomena, but as genuine expressions of faith. Such respect should be concretely integrated and reflected in the church's evangelization and mission. All religions are arenas of honest seeking of God. And surely, such seeking cannot be seen as totally in vain. Generally, it does not make much sense to try to turn other religions into more or less bleak copies of Christianity. This is a possible outcome of some versions of dialogue theology. Other religious faiths must rather be valued on the basis of their own integrity and self-understanding. And as dialogue partners, adherents to such faiths are our equals in all respects.

Today, it is a sad fact that religious convictions are often at the center of acute human conflicts. This has led to strong prejudices, particularly over against Islam. However, militant religious intolerance or regular terrorism should not be regarded primarily as religious phenomena, but rather as results of socio-political constellations. At any rate, such attitudes must not be allowed to conceal or invalidate the promise of religion in promoting human reconciliation — not least in view of our efforts to remove the fear that leads to intolerance. The ministry of reconciliation in a divided world is fundamental to the church. In the present situation, one of the most important requirements of this ministry is constructive exchange across religious and cultural barriers. A materialist spirituality is capable of contributing significantly to such exchange.

Literature

Ahmed, Akbar, and Brian Frost, eds. *After Terror: Promoting Dialogue Among Civilizations.* Cambridge: Polity Press, 2005.

Bell, Catherine. *Ritual: Perspectives and Dimensions.* New York: Oxford University Press, 1997.

Bosch, David. *Transforming Mission: Paradigm Shifts in Theology of Mission,* new edition. Maryknoll, NY: Orbis Books, 1992.

Carmody, Denise Lardner, and John Tully Carmody. *Prayer in World Religions.* Maryknoll, NY: Orbis Books, 1990.

Fitzgerald, Michael, and John Borelli. *Interfaith Dialogue: A Catholic View.* London: SPCK, 2006.

15 Concluding Remarks

A Living Hope — a Hope for Life

In the preceding chapters, I have hopefully been able to explain what is meant by the perhaps still slightly strange concept of a "materialist spirituality." We are here talking about a diverse entity that relates to several aspects of our faith life. In concluding this account, I would like to reiterate some of my key points:

1. At the outset, materialist spirituality is conceived as a critical spirituality. It contains critical perspectives on the situation within the churches, on the current religious market, and on political and cultural developments. Here it is a crucial premise that constructive criticism promotes growth.
2. A materialist spirituality presumes that outward forms, acts, and objects are fully capable of carrying inner spiritual substance. It is therefore anchored in empirical perception — i.e., in what we see and hear, taste and smell. In that sense, it is a "democratic spirituality" open to all.
3. Theologically speaking, materialist spirituality is grounded in the Trinity — or more precisely in God's work as creator, in the incarnation of Christ, and in the practical life-giving activity of the Holy Spirit. Here it is a main concern that creation and redemption belong together in God's plan of salvation and must thus also be kept firmly together in our spiritual life.
4. Materialist spirituality is not lived out in an abstract spiritualized vacuum, but in the concrete — and interconnected — spaces of

      church and world. Sacramentality and the sacraments are particularly important in holding these two spaces together; mediating real communion with God in Christ through elements from the created earth. This has a vast number of consequences in regard to liturgy and service, ecumenics and ethics, etc.

5. Materialist spirituality is meant as a spirituality for reality and our daily life. It deviates from all sorts of religious escapism. And being attached to plain empirical sensation, the church's sign language, and physical objects, it is accessible even when life is at the most miserable depths of despair — without presupposing a devoutness that only few of us can produce.

In this connection, the point is neither high church fancies and an exalted ecclesiology, nor a politicized theology. My version of a materialist spirituality is grounded in the richness of the Catholic tradition, but I still hope that this concept will come across as ecumenically valid. I therefore welcome all proposals to widen and strengthen its ecumenical relevance. What is at stake here is the plain and concrete realities of our faith life in God's world. Materialist spirituality is practiced or lived ecclesiology. It tries to show how the "religion of the heart" can be lived out in the public sphere. It is a piety that aims at escaping from the dead-ends of private internalization as well as ecstatic religious feelings. And even if I realize that this may be a rather tall order, my aim is to sketch a *functioning* spirituality — a spirituality that can help us live a true Christian life in our daily existence and the world at large.

Materialist spirituality is truly materialist in the sense that it is anchored in a concrete *materia* or "stuff" and in the world. There is, however, one area where the material "stuff-character" and concrete texture of this piety is put in a different light or even surpassed: Our life in Christ is *eschatological* in its nature; and it has transcendent features. This implies that faith also is focused on God's future with us, that it contains a hope which applies across time, and that it takes us beyond the present realm. While the requirement of sound down-to-earth spirituality remains, we must keep in mind the obvious fact that those who continually have both feet planted on the ground stand still.

      Christian life is always lived out within a dialectical relationship — or a tension — between "already" and "not yet," between what is now and what will come. This is the main background of Paul's statement that "we walk by faith, not by sight" (2 Cor. 5:7). Our hope is grounded in invisible realities: ". . . for the things that are seen are transient, but the things that are unseen are eternal" (2 Cor. 4:18). Moreover, "in . . . hope we were saved. Now, hope that is seen is not hope. For who hopes for what he sees? But if we hope for what we do not see, we wait for it with patience" (Rom. 8:24-25). This also lies behind the inescapable ambivalence that marks our life in Christ and the fatiguing restlessness that comes with it. Such sentiments can be hard to endure. Yet, they may be preferable to spiritualized complacency. Personally, I have come to realize that I need a certain amount of spiritual anxiety in order to stay alert. Thus, I dare to pray: Do not take this unrest away from me.

However, eschatology does not pertain solely to a distant future. The eschatological realm and its forces broke forth when the Son of God entered our world. These forces will accompany us until Christ's work is completed. And they will guide us into the consummated kingdom of God. In a similar way, transcendence can be seen as the fulfillment of immanence and therefore as something that presupposes and builds upon immanent realities. Accordingly, our hope is not directed towards something entirely novel or unseen, but towards the renewal or restitution of the world and the redemption of creation. God's plan of salvation will not be completed before Christ returns in victory. But still: Salvation is not only a future thing; it is available here and now.

In the wake of this, it must be underscored that even if our hope in Christ transcends our earthly life, it clearly also applies to this life. The most central asset of this hope is that it is capable of offering us a share in the future God has prepared for us already now. It therefore carries its fulfillment in itself. In the scriptures, Christian hope is described along these lines:

> Blessed be the God and Father of our Lord Jesus Christ! By his great mercy we have been born anew to a living hope through the resurrection of Jesus Christ from the dead, and to an inheritance which is imperishable, undefiled, and unfading, kept in heaven for you, who by God's power are guarded through faith for a salvation ready to be revealed in the last time. (1 Peter 1:3-5)

191

As a living hope, our hope in Christ must also be a hope for life. It connects us with the primary life-giving event, namely Christ's resurrection. We have already "been born anew" to it. Even if it is "kept in heaven," it is "imperishable . . . and unfading." And since God never fails to keep any of his promises to us, there is nothing in this world that can ever rock or invalidate our hope.

The hope that is a hope for life can only be lived out fully within one context — namely God's world. Once more, there is no room for false escapism. Our hope is a two-way link between an occasionally gloomy everyday existence and the ultimate fulfillment in Christ, between our troubled world and the renewed heaven and earth we wait for. Thus seen, Christian hope becomes a crucial constituent of a materialist spirituality. And even if it is basically invisible, it can and must be visualized and concretized. This happens in and through our life in Christ as a whole. But also here the church's sacramental celebration and its focus on earthly elements play a key role. The bread and wine of the Eucharist are tokens of the redemption of creation.

In today's culture, Christian eschatology is squeezed between neo-religious escapism that resembles former "pie in the sky" attitudes and the spreading of violent apocalyptic myths. Both these currents are selling, but the latter seems to be in the lead right now — not least due to outrageous TV series, films, and computer games. This implies that even the Apocalypse has been turned into a piece of entertainment. I am no expert on the just-mentioned genres, but I dare to assume that they are not exactly helpful in getting a grip on reality. In the wake of this, hope too is squeezed. There may be loads of unreal and dreamy aspirations around these days, but little viable and sound hope. And those who need hope most — i.e., the suffering, oppressed, and deprived, are brusquely stripped of it. At any rate, real hope has become an endangered species, while hopelessness is spreading like a plague. This plague is extremely dangerous. For how can we keep up a life worth living if we cease to hope?

Hope cannot be rekindled through vain expectations and false consolation. Georg Henrik von Wright, a Finnish philosopher and former associate of Ludwig Wittgenstein, is therefore correct in suggesting that the illusory hopes we frequently adhere to must be unveiled and de-masked. At the same time, an inclination towards hopelessness is an even greater challenge today. In this connection, von Wright speaks about the need for an active and critical *provocative pessimism* that can counteract the *futile optimism* or regular vanity we tend to cling to. This particularly applies to the immense environmental problems we are facing. And the key point is that only a soundly *realistic hope* will be sustainable on the long run.

Here we are confronted with a highly complex task. And I shall not claim that our Christian hope can deliver an ultimate and complete response to this challenge on its own. In our efforts to identify a viable hope for the world, constructive cooperation with all persons of good will — irrespective of religious convictions — is required. Moreover, our hope in Christ does not invalidate true human aspirations. Still, this hope has something special to offer in this field:

First, Christian hope is firmly grounded in the creator's steadfast faithfulness to his creation and in the process initiated by Christ that will lead to the earth's redemption. Further, God's care for every one of us is boundless. This suggests that, in the final instance, a humanity and a world whose foundation is God can only find their real meaning — or true self-realization — in seeking God and somehow remaining in his hand. Thus, hope becomes a way home for all of us. Or to express it in the words of the psalmist: "For God alone my soul waits in silence; from him comes my salvation" (Ps. 62:1).

Second, the church is summoned to be a visible concretization of our hope in Christ in and for the world. It is called to be a community of hope, of living hope, in a world that desperately needs such hope. This presupposes that the people of God will succeed in standing forth as an effective sign of the ultimate goal and content of our hope, namely the kingdom of God. And as already indicated, this kingdom is a place where the last become first and where the smallest are the greatest. This differs distinctly from the world we have shaped, but it is fully in keeping with the aim and will of the creator.

Third, Christian hope is a hope for life. But it also transcends our present existence. It even challenges death, "the last enemy" (1 Cor. 15:26). Along these lines, hope in Christ proposes an answer to one of our greatest and most distressing enigmas: Is death the end, or can we hope for something else and something more? In hope we believe that "death is swallowed up in victory" (1 Cor. 15:54). This process began when Christ defeated the powers of death at the cross, and it will be completed in view of all forms of life when he returns. It is our obligation to share this hope with everybody.

In our Christian existence as a whole, hope plays an indispensable role. Life in faith is a life in hope, and life in hope is a life in faith. Our hope in Christ even provides for its own defense. It includes forces and fosters attitudes that can keep it alive against all odds and all calculations of probability. In this connection, Karl Rahner speaks about something he calls *the grace of perseverance:*

> . . . we are asking a theological question about ourselves which is the question of perseverance. To raise the theological question of perseverance is the same thing as to ask whether or not a person will finally be what he now is or at least hopes to be.
>
> [. . .]
>
> The strange thing that immediately presents itself when it comes to questioning the essence and origin of perseverance is that, on the one hand, our future will certainly be worked out by our freedom, and that, on the other hand, we are completely in the hand of God. Only when a person has experienced, believed, feared, and loved God in the absolute surrender of his whole being — and therefore also of his whole future, can he begin to realize the full meaning of God's power and freedom. We can only live in close contact with God when we believe in Him as the only true love, and when we accept our future from Him as a gift which, as the result of our own freedom, still really belongs to God.
>
> [. . .]
>
> Therefore, our first conclusion with regard to perseverance is: Our heart can be composed and serene only in God's grace, and it can only attain serenity if it is restless in the love of God. We are not seized by a suspicious fear when we are with someone we truly love. Perfect love drives out fear. But we can also say: Perfect love effects a holy fear of God that renders us happy, calm, and confident.
>
> [. . .] If we were to ask ourselves whether or not there are signs of belonging to God's "elect," we would have to say that there are no signs, such as legal documents, that can be adduced as proof of certain perseverance in grace. If there are any signs of election, then

they can only be those effected by our own actions, which are signs that God is working in us. Such signs are, for example, constancy in prayer, steady progress in doing good, God-fearing concern for salvation, selfless love, and so forth. We might also mention those special experiences a person has that lead him on gently and irresistibly so that, amazed, he asks himself occasionally how he escaped this or that disaster; or he might ask himself how he was able to accomplish certain things for which there was really no indication in his physical and psychological make-up.

[. . .]

. . . In any event, we should have trust in God, we should lovingly do right now what we can, we should begin with our program as soon as possible, and recognize in our love for the Mother of God and the Heart of Christ an assurance that we are still open for the love of God. If we can do that, then love can drive out fear, and we can go forward to meet God with an open heart, thankfully and joyously, calmly and also without a detailed knowledge of our future. Then it will be clear that "He who began the good work in you is faithful, and will bring His work to completion." (*Spiritual Exercises*, pp. 278-85)

The grace of perseverance is of particular relevance in our daily lives; it is a vital contribution to "a spirituality for reality." Here we need a piety that also works in hard and evil times. Not least within contexts like these our hope must prove its sustainability. However, such sustainability has become a firm reality in the lives of a vast number of our Christian sisters and brothers — across time as well as space, often in far worse situations than many of us find ourselves in. And it is also fully feasible that we shall experience our hope in Christ carrying us — not around, but directly through whatever anguish may come.

What has been said so far affirms that our Christian hope is of essential significance to a materialist spirituality. One might even suggest that hope constitutes the "soul" of the physical stuff that such piety is built from. It further enables us to maintain a silent but crystal-clear tone of hope even in the gloomiest of days. It is vital in responding to the hopelessness of our fellow human beings. And it keeps us attentive to the renewed heaven and earth, without in any sense forgetting or abandoning the world we live in.

On the one hand, materialist spirituality will barely be able to survive without hope. On the other hand, a hope that loses the solid foundation such piety contributes will easily degenerate into floating aspirations or pure vanity. A viable hope needs a sound footing; without such footing, it may be turned into mere "pie in the sky." Thus seen, these entities clearly belong together; they are in a sense two sides of the same coin. A "secular" version of the dialectic between "materialism" and hope can be found in writings of the German neo-Marxist philosopher Ernst Bloch. Not least, Jürgen Moltmann's theology is influenced by Bloch. Within the framework of a materialist spirituality, the point is that we become "rooted and grounded in love" through visible signs and a partly invisible hope. In this way, "we may have power to comprehend with all the saints what is the breadth and length and height and depth; and to know the love of Christ which surpasses knowledge, that you may be filled with all the fullness of God" (Eph. 3:17-19). This directs us towards a spirituality that is committed to the world while having a vision of the infinite — or tastes of heaven while smelling freshly of earth.

Hope and faith are complementary entities; faith underpins hope, and hope invigorates faith. Moreover, just as our life-giving faith is not meant to drag us away from the world, our living hope in Christ is anything but escapist. It rather helps us to master an occasionally complicated world — also carrying a promise for the world to come. Hope is our unyielding protest song against oppression and suffering, illness and death, sin and devil. Simultaneously, it is our equally firm song of consolation when life becomes hard. And it goes like this: Glory to God in the highest, he who even "the highest heaven cannot contain" (2 Chron. 6:18). But also: Glory to God in the lowest, he who "(dwells) . . . with him who is of a contrite and humble spirit" (Isa. 57:15). This conspicuous mixture of highness and lowness is fundamental to our Christian hope.

Through hope we get a foretaste of and a share in the kingdom of God in its fullness, while being firmly grounded on earth. In chapter 3, I quoted the breathtaking vision of Revelation 21:1-5, of the new heaven and the new earth where God "will wipe away every tear from [our] eyes, and death shall be no more" (v. 4). Here I refer to its continuation, depicting "the new Jerusalem":

. . . I saw no temple in the city, for its temple is the Lord God the Almighty and the Lamb. And the city has no need of sun or moon to shine upon it, for the glory of God is its light, and its lamp is the Lamb. By its lights shall the nations walk; and the kings of the earth shall bring their glory into it, and its gates shall never be shut by day — and there shall be no night there; they shall bring into it the glory and the honor of the nations. But nothing unclean shall enter it, nor any one who practices abomination or falsehood, but only those who are written in the Lamb's book of life.

Then he showed me the river of the water of life, bright as crystal, flowing from the throne of God and of the Lamb through the middle of the street of the city; also, on either side of the river, the tree of life with its twelve kinds of fruit, yielding its fruit each month; and the leaves of the tree were for the healing of the nations. There shall no more be anything accursed, but the throne of God and of the Lamb shall be in it, and his servants shall worship him; they shall see his face, and his name shall be on their foreheads. And night shall be no more; they need no light of lamp or sun, for the Lord God will be their light, and they shall reign for ever and ever. (Rev. 21:22–22:5)

How different and extra-terrestrially beautiful this sounds. But at the same time, the just-quoted vision strikes a note that reminds us of the best moments of our earthly life. Like a bright and tender summer night in the mountains. Like the gently falling snow of winter. Like a music recital that opens up new dimensions. Like the experience of fellowship with those who are closest to us, an experience that fills us with deep joy. Or like moments in God's house, the church, where we sense that the Eucharist carries us and the liturgy lifts us — without being dragged into outer space. This is perhaps a sign that a materialist spirituality may be a piety not only for the present realm, but also for eternity.

Literature

Bloch, Ernst. *The Principle of Hope,* paperback edition. Cambridge, MA: MIT Press, 1986.

Kelly, Anthony. *Eschatology and Hope.* Maryknoll, NY: Orbis Books, 2006.

Moltmann, Jürgen. *Theology of Hope,* new edition. London: SCM, 2002.

Rahner, Karl. *Spiritual Exercises*, 3rd impression. London: Sheed & Ward, 1976.

Volf, Miroslav, and William Katerberg, eds. *The Future of Hope: Christian Tradition amid Modernity and Postmodernity*. Grand Rapids: Eerdmans, 2004.

Index